The Ciner

© 1981 J. Barker R. Brown

ISBN 0 903852 15 2

Printed by Princo B.V. Culemborg, the Netherlands.

Published by
Milestone Publications
62 Murray Road
Horndean
Hants PO8 9JL

Sponsored by
HOMELINE
The Nationwide Home Selling Service.
"The real alternative to estate agents. And their fees"

The Dream Palaces of Portsmouth

The audience sat spellbound, their faces illuminated by the glow of light being emitted from the great screen before them, they were witnessing the wonders of moving pictures. The year was 1909, the splendid building in which the entertainment was taking place was the old Victoria Hall, and it was packed with small bodies who had eagerly paid their pennies to pile into the hall for the traditional Saturday afternoon matinee.

But there was a few adults scattered amongst the audience, subjecting their eardrums to the occasional cries of excitement from the youngsters. The programme had been under way about fifteen minutes when a lady happened to glance towards the projection box. To her horror she saw flames leaping from the equipment. Without thinking she immediately panicked, jumping to her feet, she gave forth a shout of "Fire"! This action prompted hundreds of children to rush for the exit doors, creating bedlam in their anxiety to escape from the building.

The cinema staff appealed to the patrons to keep calm, but it was to no avail. Up in the gallery one of the attendants named Ellis tried his utmost to assure the 200 filmgoers that they would come to no harm if they did not panic. Then he saw that one of the guard rails was yeilding to the pressure of the bodies, he fought his way over to it and held it in place. But a young hooligan, on finding his way barred, struck Mr. Ellis with a bottle, knocking this gentleman to the floor. Immediately the rail gave way, causing scores of children to topple over the balcony edge.

The bodies fell like leaves from a tree, landing in a sprawling mass in the stalls below. To their credit, throughout this melee, the orchestra continued to play their instruments as if an outbreak of fire was an every day occurrence. Indeed, the fire was not that bad, and although the gallery was closed, a performance was given in the evening as usual. But the stampede for safety had taken its toll, apart from the many youngsters that were injured that afternoon, there was one 11-year old lad who would never go to the pictures again, he was crushed to death.

That horrific incident happened on the 14th of August, 1909, and it is just a small chapter in the history of cinema going in the Portsmouth area. We are pleased to be able to report that many of the other incidents that took place are of a more happy type, for after all, that is what going to the pictures is all about, to enjoy yourselves.

With the type and quality of films that are being produced today, it may well be argued that modern film-makers have lost sight of this factor. Enjoyable entertainment should be the order of the day, and this can rarely be achieved by showing films in bad taste containing an over indulgence of violence and bad language. This type of fare was shown all too often in the 1970s. (Perhaps this is because of the times we live in, the cinema has always kept abreast of the times.) Back in the 20s and 30s times were more depressing than violent, and so movie-makers attempted to bring people out of their doldrums. For this they produced happy-go-lucky musicals with little or no story, and you can be sure if there was some semblance of a story, the good guy always won the girl, the patron always went home happy!

In a way this was rather incongruous, the filmgoer would be subjected to scenes of the screen idols romping in opulent surroundings, lounging by private swimming pools, cuddling well groomed pooches wearing diamond studded collars, or wandering through their 40-bedroomed mansions. Then the cinema patron would return to his rented two-up, two-down, straight off the pavement abode, swig back a mug of "Epps'" cocoa, crawl into a bug-infested bed, and doze-off no doubt dreaming that tomorrow may be the day he finds a job!

And still we yearned for news about our favourites, rushing down to the corner shop early on Saturday mornings to make sure we got a copy of the 'Picture Show' magazine. On thumbing through the pages with eager fingers we discover that 'Like 9 out of 10 other film stars, Madeleine Carroll uses Lux Toilet Soap to keep her skin satin smooth'. But I am afraid at 4d. a bar, we shall have to carry on using our Mum's best carbolic! And what is this we read, Tom Mix is to marry for the fifth time. No doubt he wishes his real life wives would keep silent like his heroines on the screen!

Maybe it was all rather foolish, standing in front of the dressing table mirror pouting our lips just as Jean Harlow had done in "Hell's Angels", or wrapping Mum's best scarf round our heads and brandishing Dad's walking stick, pretending we were Doug Fairbanks in the "Black Pirate". Sheer escapism! But **where else** than the dear old pictures could you escape from your environment for a couple of hours, all for the cost of a few **coppers**. In that two hours ladies may have imagined that it was **actually** themselves that Rudolph Valentino was scooping up from the desert sand to carry away on his white Arabian steed. And then, home to reality! There is your spouse snoring in front of the kitchen range with open mouth and false teeth just sliding over his lower lip, not a pretty sight after seeing the handsome Rudolph! Never mind, have a cup of cocoa. "Epps'" of course!

Even the picture palaces themselves were made to impart a feeling of grandeur to their patrons, if the buildings did not convey this, their names certainly did! Hence titles such as the Savoy, Regent, Ritz, Palace, Majestic, Ambassador, Apollo, Princes, Plaza or the Queen's. And so as you passed through the portals of these places of pleasure, it is easy to understand that you may have had the feeling that you were entering somewhere special. In the foyer you were very often met by a marble gold-fish pond, surrounded by pillars and potted palms. Inside the auditorium the ceilings were sometimes studded with twinkling lights, giving the impression that you were watching the films out in the open by starlight.

The cinema staff also entered into the show-biz spirit, dressed in resplendent uniforms, ready to usher folk to their seats or sell ice-creams during the intervals. Some of these were very eager to please, just one example is the cinema where an usherette in the form of a grey-haired old lady showed you to your seat, if you had come in after the film had started she would sit down next to you and whisper a quick run through of what had happened so far in the plot!

The staff were very often ruled over by a sergeant-major type gentleman who always wore his war medals proudly displayed across the chest of his coat, he could also prove quite formidable when it came to keeping the kids quiet during the afternoon matinees. Also keeping up the show-biz tradition, to promote certain mammoth productions, the cinema staff would discard their uniforms for more colourful attire. For instance, when the 1937 classic "Victoria the Great" with Anna Neagle was showing, patrons could expect to be met in the foyer by an usherette actually dressed in a gown that was used in the film by Anna. With some of the films being made nowadays, the mind boggles at how the staff would dress, or undress, if this idea was resurrected!

But cinemas have always been very publicity conscious, especially with trailers for forthcoming attractions. Have you ever noticed that the film that is showing next week always looks better than the one you are seeing this week? And when you go and see it next week, the one on the following week looks better again!

To further the cause of publicity, all sorts of stunts were tried to advertise shows. Albert Jacobs was a publicity agent in the Portsmouth area back in the silent movie days, and one of his favourite stunts for attracting publicity was to dress up in convict gear and ride around the area in a van looking much like a Black Maria. It would stop in a crowded thoroughfare, and

Albert would leap out the back and start running as if he had escaped, followed by chaps dressed as warders. They would catch him, and after a crowd had gathered to see what was going on, they would suddenly produce handbills to advertise a show!

This stunt went down very well in Portsmouth, but they came unstuck over in Gosport. The van stopped in the High Street, Albert jumped out and started to run a few yards, for he was stopped in his tracks by a huge Marine from Forton Barracks. Thinking he was rendering a public service, the Marine delivered a beautiful upper-cut to Albert's jaw to lay him out on the pavement. Albert came back to consciousness in hospital, and vowed never to pull the convict stunt again!

There was always great competition between the various cinemas, and in their individual advertising they used to adopt slogans to push the merits of going into their establishment. Hence statements on billboards proclaiming "Always Cozy and Warm", "The Family House", or "If its a good picture, its coming here".

And if the cinema had just been decorated, or perhaps refurbished with new seats, they were always quick to point this out, as if their establishment was the cleanest joint in town. But the patrons still called them "Fleapits", or "Bughutches"! And it did not exactly infuse confidence when an attendant came round during the intervals to spray a foul smelling liquid over the tops of our heads, giving the reminder that it was not only some of the films that were lousy in those days! When you got home, there was no use denying to Mum that you had been to the pictures, the disinfectant would linger on your bonce for days!

Managements always strove to be first at anything, whether it was a wonderous new form of cinematic equipment or a piece of newsreel showing topical happenings in the great wide world outside Portsmouth. Relating to the newsreels, they would very often be shared by two cinemas in the same chain. This explained the sight of young lads peddling like fury with cans of film on their bikes between the picture houses, and more than once the programmes would be delayed because the rider had come off his bike, strewing film across the tramlines!

Another story relating to the interchange of films concerns the Criterion cinema in Gosport, and the old Alexandra in Fareham. At one time they were both owned by William Bonwick, and his name crops up fairly often in Portsmouth cinema history as you will read later. Anyway, Bill had a nice little fiddle going with the tram and bus crews on the Gosport to Fareham route to transport film between the Criterion and the Alexandra. The film would be picked up outside one cinema then dropped off at the other, and so it went on all day, back and forth on the route. Unfortunately, one day an inspector stayed on the tram at Fareham, and the driver could not deliver the film, so back it went to Gosport! The poor audience in the Alexandra would be left watching a blank screen until the film came back on the next tram!

Nearly every cinema boasted its own orchestra in the old days, although it was quite likely you would see the same musicians appear in different cinemas, a great deal of moonlighting went on. There was also a fairly wide definition of the word 'orchestra', this could mean a 10-piece ensemble, or one solitary pianist! Mind you, some of those pianists could sound like a ten-piece at times, thumping away on the keyboard as if there were no tomorrow!

A great favourite for accompanying the silent films was "The Overture to William Tell", marvellous for action movies with chase scenes. Imagine what it was like when "Ben Hur" was shown, there was the evil Francis X. Bushman driving his chariot, holding the reins with one hand and whipping handsome Ramon Novarro with the other. This gave the pianist of 1926 a chance to go berserk, and the piano keys probably got more of a hammering than Ramon!

4

Yes, the pianists had a melody for every mood. When the heroine was being cast out into the snow with her baby in her arms, this was the moment for a plaintive rendering of "Hearts and Flowers". And of course when the hero Handsome Jack leaped onto the scene to save her from being decapitated by a speeding express train, this called for a rousing "My Hero" from the "Chocolate Soldier"!

In later years the cinema organ took over the musical parts in the programme, this gave us the view of the back of shiney-domed gents emerging from out of the bowels of the earth, sitting astride the stool of their giant Wurlitzers. It was quite understandable that many of us actually believed that the little man lived in a small room below the cinema stage.

Anyway, it was not long before we would all be singing along with him, following the little white ball! The Shaftesbury in Kingston Road was one of the first picture houses in the Portsmouth area that could boast an organ on the premises and of course this instrument was of the church type. Marvellous for creating suitable mood music for films that included stately scenes with royalty and such like, but the organ did not have the versatility that later models in the 30s could provide.

One of the first cinema organs in Portsmouth that was purpose built for the job was at the Regent Cinema in North End - later to become the Gaumont. That organ was installed in 1928, and of course this was an important period in the history of the cinema; with the coming of the 'talkies' the organ took on another role. Instead of being used for accompaniment, they provided live music between the films. This heralded a new wave or organists, many of whom became household names. One of these was Reginald Porter Brown, and he in fact played for the opening of the Savoy in Commercial Road in 1937, his nimble fingers performed musical miracles on what was billed as the "Compton Wonder Organ". These organists always appeared to have the same format: after rising from the depths to a solitary spotlight, they would commence their short programme with a stirring piece, then lapse into a rather classical type of number as if to prove that they were capable of better things, and then finally wake the audience up again with a good selection of sing-along tunes. At the end, amidst thunderous applause, they would turn and wave a cheery farewell with a promise to be back next week, then disappear back from whence they had come!

Cinemas were more than just glittering places of amusement. They were part of our lives. Where we spent our childhood, where we did our courting and perhaps stole our first kiss from a freckle-faced lass with her hair tied in bunches, where we crowded together with others to take our minds off the bombs falling outside.

Relating to the cinema in wartime, it is understandable that many who lived through those dreadful years have always nourished the feeling that the picture houses were one of our biggest weapons against Hitler's evil machine. They certainly brought out a burst of patriotism that has been unparalleled since, especially in the newsreels. Film of captured German or Italian prisoners of war sullenly marching with their hands above their heads would produce spontaneous applause from the cinema audience!

Even with the wartime films containing a strong propaganda content, we were still glad to go three times a week. Most of the picture places had three changes of programme: Sundays, Monday to Wednesday and Thursday to Saturday. We cheered through such filmfare as "Target for Tonight", "Western Approaches", "Desert Victory". We listened intently to the ministerial shorts warning us that "Careless Talk Costs Lives", or advising us how to stretch our meagre food rations.

Of course, when America entered the war scene, Hollywood employed an entirely different approach. True enough, at the end of many of the films they proclaimed "Buy War Bonds", but some of the mock heroics leading up to that end were very hard to accept. We were usually treated to Big John Wayne standing upright in the middle of a battlefield with shells dropping all round him, his gigantic frame adorned with what appeared to be at least 200 hand grenades, urging his gum chewing comrades to follow him 'over the top'. Or an M.G.M. pilot at the controls of a fighter plane diving at an alarming speed towards an enemy aircraft carrier, whilst with great determination our hero spits these glorious lines: "Okay you dirty Japs, you killed my best buddy, now you are going to get yours". But I am afraid when Errol Flynn showed how he won the war in the east with "Objective Burma" in 1945, the British could not take it and the film was banned!

Cinemas were closed at the outbreak of war, but it did not take long for them to open again, and it was soon a common sight to see long queues encircling the exteriors, patrons sometimes having to wait outside throughout a whole programme. Usherettes of that period must have developed eyes like owls, for in 1940 it was revealed that many of them in the Portsmouth area were working 67 hours a week!

Yes, the people of Portsmouth were truly film fiends, eagerly awaiting their weekly dose of celluloid wonder. Lets go back to the early days when it all began, in fact back before actual picture houses were built for such entertainment.

The showing of films around the turn of the century was really a travelling affair, more like a fairground booth, but as the films and the equipment for showing them improved, local halls were hired. Proprietors of cinematic entertainment such as "Poole's Myriorama" would pay regular visits. Meeting places such as the Victoria Hall in Portsmouth, the Star Assembly Rooms in Gosport, or the Portland Hall in Fareham were booked. For weeks prior to the visits pennies would be saved, and on the great day many eager little bodies with grubby hands clutching their entrance fee would descend upon the hall, their wonder of what they were seeing was enough to make them forget that the benches they had to sit on were pretty hard for small bottoms, not forgetting the splinters!

Portsmouth can be proud that one of her sons was one of the pioneers of living pictures, he was known as the 'Grandfather of Films' and his name was Alfred West. He began his working career in the family photographic business that had been started by his father. They had branches at Gosport and later Palmerston Road, Southsea. One of Alfred's technical claims to fame in the photographic world was the invention of the instantaneous shutter, enabling objects to be photographed in motion. In the 1880s he was the first to capture a photograph of a sailing boat in full sail.

But Alfred had his interest drawn towards the wonder of moving films, his first effort of note in this field was "Our Navy", which of course was a very natural subject for the area we live in. The film was a tremendous success, not only in Portsmouth, where it had as it were a captive audience, but also throughout the whole country. And probably for what was the first Royal Command Film Performance: Queen Victoria requested that it was shown at Osborne House.

In the following years moving pictures enjoyed increasing success, made popular by such chaps as West. But in 1914, after returning from Australia, Alfred West sold his interests. After the war he moved to the Isle of Wight and bought a small farm where he cultivated violets, in fact he became quite famous all over again. After his wife died he moved back to the mainland, where he died in 1937 at the age of 80 in a Southsea nursing home.

Harry Cook was one of the early cinema pioneers in Portsmouth, he started in 1908 with his travelling film show at the

Kingsley Hall in Southsea, where he played for two weeks. He then toured the area, the audiences were so enthusiastic with the new wonder, Harry had no difficulty in convincing them that the very badly scratched film represented rainstorms! In later years when the business became more respectable, Harry became the well known proprietor of the Shaftesbury in Kingston Road, helped by his sister Miss V. Cook.

And so, as the popularity of the moving film increased, it was evident that more permanent buildings were required in which to hold the entertainment. Picture houses sprouted up all over the country, and dear old Portsmouth certainly had its fair share of these establishments.

The film going public embarked on a love affair that was to last almost fifty years, at least until that square lantern that most of us have in our living rooms was to really take hold. When we see some of those old films from the distant past shown on television, one is sometimes apt to reflect: "Gosh, did I actually pay money to see that at one time".

But of course, apart from some of the stinkers, and there were plenty of those, there were several movies with magic moments that have remained implanted in our memory boxes for all time. Many will have their own particular favourites, it may have been when Valentino gave his seductive and smouldering sneer as "The Sheik" in 1921, or when the resonant tones of Al Jolson came bursting from the screen in 1927 with "The Jazz Singer". Perhaps when we saw the first glimpse of Boris Karloff as the Frankenstein monster appear round the door; when Paul Robeson's glorious voice was heard singing the Canoe Song in "Sanders of the River"; Errol Flynn as Robin Hood running his sword through the evil Sir Guy played by Basil Rathbone; Charles Laughton as Quasimodo launching his grotesque frame upon the bells in "Hunchback of Notre Dame"; the cherubic Shirley Temple capturing our hearts in "Little Miss Marker".

The memories go on and on!

If we still retain fond thoughts of our favourite movies, it is just as likely that we have the same about some of the old cinemas in which we spent our youth, most of which have by now been demolished to make way for supermarkets or blocks of offices, or maybe turned into a bingo hall.

And that is really what this is all about, the old cinemas of the Portsmouth area. The subject is so vast, and so varied, it is almost impossible to mention every picture house that ever existed. Having said that, we hope to produce more than has ever been written before about our area's dream palaces.

The easy way out would be to present a list of the cinemas, and a few facts on their history. But I am afraid this would not make very entertaining reading. And so, after much deliberation, we invite you to come with us upon a cinema crawl, not a pub crawl, although these places of alcoholic delight might rear their bleary heads occasionally throughout our nostalgic wanderings!

Right! Are you ready? Then off we shall jolly well go! But don't forget to pay your sixpence to the lady in the box-office, and please promise that you will share your bag of popcorn!

The Journey Begins

So there you are! So glad you decided to join us on this nostalgic stroll. Where are we? Well, have a good look around you. Even better, look up. You will see clues such as Gladstone or Pearl Buildings, planted on ornate and rather splendid examples of architecture. Need I remind you that trams rumble past at frequent intervals, for one of Portsmouth's longest roads begins at this point.

That's right, dear old Commercial Road. Where better to start our cinematic jaunt, for nearby was one of the country's first cinemas. In 1885 that magnificent structure known as Gladstone

Buildings was erected, another work of art that could be attributed to that fine Portsmouth architect, A.E. Cogswell, whose work featured so prominently in the city. Gladstone Buildings was built on the site of Hampshire House, which had formerly served as a residence for an officer of the Garrison.

Victoria Hall was part of the Buildings, a popular venue for meetings and for presenting exhibitions. It was here that the pioneers of moving pictures came to demonstrate their latest wonders to an eager public, a picture house was to evolve on this site that would draw patrons for sixty years.

The Victoria Hall Cinema

One of the first cinema shows in Britain was presented at the Victoria Hall in 1896, in July of that year an entertainment known as Cinematoscope was presented. It was described as animated photographs, all as in life! The posters proclaimed that if the patron paid the sum of 6d. he could see dancers dancing, and boxers boxing! Which makes one wonder what else dancers and boxers would do! Anyway, these shows were presented half-hourly which was not very good value for sixpence even in those days. You could probably have had a three-course meal and a pint for sixpence!

However, in the following month of August in 1896, a much improved cinematic programme was provided. This was billed as "Paul's Original and Only Theatrograph", direct from the Alhambra Theatre in London. Five performances daily were given at the Victoria Hall, and the public flocked in to see such items of film interest as "The Prince of Wales' Horse Winning the Derby", "Princess Maud's Wedding" and "Pictures of Spanish Life". Need we add that this created much excitement amongst the audiences that paid the entrance fee, you must remember that this took place only eight months after the first public exhibition of moving pictures had been given by the Lumiere Cinematographe in Paris.

Interior - Victoria Hall

In the following five years the showing of films at the hall was rather spasmodic, then in 1900 a young chap named Arthur Andrews hired the Victoria Hall for the regular showing of films. At £60 per week for the hire of the hall this would seem to have been quite a risk, but Arthur had great faith, also a great push from his dear wife, who was reputed to be a lady with plenty of business acumen.

Andrews' first presentation took place on March the 26th 1900. It was "Our Navy". This you will recall I mentioned previously, a film extravaganza produced by the West family of Portsmouth photographers. It depicted life in the Navy, providing a complete picture of a sailor's life from the time he joins up. The film was silent of course, but from the side of the stage a running commentary was given by a Mr. Harry Coveney, adding a

Victoria Hall, early days
Commercial Road

wonderful touch of authenticity to the proceedings with his vocal descriptions. "Our Navy" was a huge success. There was a big demand for seats, but despite this Mr. and Mrs. Andrews still invited along a mob of kids from local orphanages for a free show. Maybe they had an eye to encouraging the filmgoers of the future.

In the following years there were several film shows at the Victoria Hall, but most of them were in the documentary vein. The South African War provided a fair amount of film coverage, raising a great deal of patriotic fever with the showing of the raising of the Union Jack at Bloomfontein. On a local note, film of Portsmouth's great welcome to Bugler Dunn, the hero of the Colenso Battle resulted in much cheering and clapping from Victoria Hall audiences.

The hall really became a full-time cinema in August 1908. Leased by the Andrews who had realized by now, thanks to their bank balance, that film shows could only improve and go from strength to strength. The prospective audiences certainly had no argument with these sentiments; they craved for more films to brighten their sometimes humdrum existence.

During the Andrews' proprietorship, two fires of note took place: the worst being the 1909 affair described at the beginning, the other happened in June 1911. After the 1909 fire Mr. Andrews was made very aware of what grave consequences a blaze could produce within a structure such as a cinema, he certainly did not want it to happen again. And so he set to and devised a rather unique safety device. This comprised a lavatory cistern mounted over the most inflammable piece of equipment, the projector. A length of string was fixed between cistern and projector, the idea being that in the event of a fire the string would burn and immediately release water from the cistern to douse the flames.

Unfortunately, on the night of the 26th of June 1911, this firefighting gadget had no effect, the water fell as planned, but it was not enough to put out the flames being emitted from a blazing spool of film. Seeing the glow from the projection room, the audience was already making a wild dash for the exit doors. But there was no need to panic, for prompt action by Mr. Andrews and his staff had the blaze under control. Both the 1909 and 1911 fire prompted letters to the local press and Watch Committee, pointing out the inadequacies of fire protection in local places of entertainment. This did eventually bring about improvements in fire precautions, notably swing doors that would allow quick access to the street outside. A requirement we now accept as normal in cinemas and theatres.

And so the Victoria Hall patrons continued to attend for their weekly dose of filmfare, impatiently waiting for the following week to see whether Pearl White had been split into two Pearl Whites by the huge blades of a sawmill in "The Perils of Pauline", this was in 1914, and the following year they went back to see Pearl's further thrilling adventures in "The Exploits of Elaine".

Talking films came to the Victoria Hall in July 1929, and at first they mixed talkies with silent films until the former took over completely. I may add that for the silent film showings, they were accompanied by the full Victoria Hall Orchestra.

This cinema was subsequently taken over by the A.B.C. chain in 1937, and just two of the many film hits of that particular year were: "The Good Earth" with Paul Muni, and "Lost Horizon" with Ronald Colman. It was also the year that Mickey Rooney hit the screen in the first of the 'Andy Hardy' series.

The Victoria Hall survived the war fairly well, considering what went on around it, but it did not survive the demolition hammer that was to strike in 1960, to make way for a block of offices. Although it had experienced a brief moment of glory in 1950 with celebrations relating to its Golden Jubilee, the Deputy Lord Mayor Frank Miles cutting a special cake to mark the occasion.

The last film shown was "Expresso Bongo". The audience departed and so the doors closed on Portsmouth's first cinema, truly a building that had played a prominent part in the lives of many of the city's residents.

The Palace

Leaving behind the Victoria Hall, let us continue on this Commercial Road ramble. On we go, past Hampshire Terrace and the Wiltshire Lamb on the corner of St. Paul's Road. Stroll on past Waltham Street and Hyde Park Road, pausing for a moment to take in the resplendent bulding on the corner that housed the offices of the Portsmouth Water Company. This structure was built in 1883 and was another of Cogswell's pieces of art, it was demolished in 1970 to make way for the Winston Churchill Avenue road plan.

Just past the Water Company we come to the building we have been heading for, and strangely enough that also has the hand of Cogswell upon it. This architect is reputed to have got his building design inspirations from his travels abroad, and looking at the magnificent facia of The Palace there is little doubt where he spent his annual hols in the early 20s. With its very distinct oriental appearance, it confirms that Cogswell had an 'Away-Day' to India. The mind boggles at what sort of a building he would have designed from a visit to Poland!

The year 1921 was notable for the film that really set Rudolph Valentino on the road to glory, this was "The Four Horsemen of the Apocalypse". But on February 21st of that year the eyes of Portsmouth's filmgoers were attracted to the opening of The Palace Theatre in Commercial Road.

Amidst swarms of local dignitaries, Mayor John Timpson performed the opening ceremony at the invitation of the proprietors, Portsmouth Cinemas Ltd. After a rabble-rousing speech he introduced the builder of the cinema, who just happened to be fellow councillor Frank Privett. For anybody in the audience who had any doubts about the strength of the building, Frank assured them that the structure contained over 250,000 bricks and one hundred tons of steelwork. Following quickly in his wake, George Woods, the Chairman of the cinema chain presented the Mayor and Mayoress with permanent passes for the cinema which he hoped they would use frequently.

The first programme shown at the Palace was "King Solomon's Mines" which played to good sized audiences that week, the capacity of the cinema being 630 persons. You could have had a seat in the stalls for 9d. or 1/3d., and if you were really flush they would let you in the Grand Circle for 2/-. In those days of the 'silents' a good orchestra was a popular attraction, and the Palace resounded to the sweet strains of select orchestral music under the baton of Mr. C.H. Martin.

With all this and the very latest trappings in the way of thick carpeted floors and lush velvet seats, it must have been a great strain to get up and leave to go home. But the Palace did have one peculiarity: it was one of those picture houses that was built back to front. The screen was behind you as one entered the stalls. This could prove most frightening. An amazon attendant would tear your ticket apart as if she was in the habit of tearing telephone directories in half before breakfast every morning, give a quick flash of her lamp to send you staggering and groping into the darkness beyond!

"Sorry, Sir! Sorry, Madam!". As your eyes get partially used to the light you can vaguely make out the forms of patrons whose laps you have just tried to sit on! Suddenly, you almost jump out of your skin as a great voice booms from behind you, "Okay, Bugsy, this is where you get yours", or maybe a rasping trumpet denoting that the United States Cavalry is just about to trample all over you! Yes, back to front type cinemas will remain firmly implanted in the memories of older patrons of the movies.

The old adverts for the programmes at the Palace were always very explicit. Perhaps they did not have the advantage of talking trailers, but they made up for this in print. The bills would have the title "Palace" in the centre with a silhouette either side of a minaret, beneath would be a description such as: "Here it is - Cowboys, Bad men, Indians, mixed with riding and shooting stunts, its a big red-blooded picture that you will revel in". That was in 1923, and it certainly helped pull in the audiences of that time. But today, with our rather blase attitudes we would probably think: "Oh, its just another cowboy film".

The dear old Palace showed its cinematic delights through the

"Palace"
Commercial Road, Portsmouth

gay 20s, the tuneful 30s, the eventful 40s and on into the television indoctrinated and dominated years of the 50s and 60s. But unlike so many of its kind that fell by the wayside, the Palace stayed in business.

This was brought about by a change in policy: the cinema had its title embellished to announce: "Palace Continental", and specialized in films of a rather more adult type. This resulted in the soundtracks emitting more grunts and groans than could normally be heard on Saturday afternoon wrestling, and the screen to overflow with young ladies of Swedish origin displaying their very ample charms, or an American lady named Chesty Morgan sporting a 72ins. bust attracting audiences of equally staggering proportions!

But regardless of what type of films it shows, the Palace is unique and must be preserved. It overcame a threat of closure in the early seventies, and we are pleased to say that in 1980 it was still in the business of showing films; although the outlook in 1981 is bleak: at the time of writing the doors are closed.

The Hippodrome

We do not have far to stroll to find our next cinema, but those with alcoholic leanings will have to force themselves past "The Yorkshire Grey" on the corner of Swan Street; whilst those with a craving for a cup of tea will have to show equal discipline to pass the Corner House Restaurant that once stood on the other corner. And then, on the corner of Salem Street we find our target: the Hippodrome.

This establishment is probably thought of more for its stage productions, but it did on various occasions, show films, so therefore we will include it as a brief respite on our journey.

The Hippodrome started its 33 years of providing entertainment to the people of Portsmouth in May 1907. It was indeed a most imposing structure from the outside, whilst on the inside it provided its patrons with the latest in luxurious trappings. In fact, the posters were not shy in their weekly list of delights to proclaim it as: "Portsmouth's Sumptuous Family Pleasure Resort".

With a frontage of 67ft. and a depth of 150ft. the establishment was capable of seating 2,000. The managing director was Walter de Frece, who was an impresario of some repute in those days, also notable for his marriage to the great Vesta Tilley. This great trooper was a regular sight on the stages of Portsmouth, belting out such classics as "Following in Father's Footsteps" or "The Army of Today's All Right".

And so, under the banner of "Portsmouth Hippodrome Ltd. this theatre in the following years presented most of the top flight performers of their day, and patrons flocked to the box-office in order to see their favourites. And of course one of those favourites, who could never do wrong in the eyes of a Pompey audience was dear old Max Miller, the Cheeky Chappie himself! This colourful comedian first appeared on the stage of the Hippodrome in 1928, the first of many such appearances.

Another artiste to pack them in that same year was Whispering Jack Smith, who at that time was reputed to be the highest paid performer in Vaudeville, needless to say he made the ladies in the audience swoon with the rendering of his latest hit song: "The Birth of the Blues".

Some of the happiest times at the Hippodrome were when the theatre gave its annual free show for the poor children of the city. At such times an endless stream of eager little urchins would pour through the doors to receive a banana, an orange, and a bag of sweets! Then they would be entertained by the Great Carmo, who always provided a grand show, the highlight of which for the kids was the appearance of Baby June, reputed to be the smallest performing elephant in the world at that time.

The list of artistes, the shows, and the stage reminiscences could seemingly go on and on! But we must get back to our objective, the cinema. Some films were shown at the Hippodrome during the 1914-18 period, although variety was still very much the main entertainment fare. Then in 1933 three hour programmes were provided, comprising two hours of variety and revue, and one hour of films.

But by the end of 1933 stage presentations once again dominated the Monday to Saturday scene, and film fans had to be content with viewing films at the Hippodrome on Sundays only, on which day a full film programme was shown.

Within eight years the Hippodrome was to suffer the fate of so many other resplendent buildings in Portsmouth, a victim of Herr Hitler's evil machine. On a January night in 1941, a period of time that will never be forgotten by Portsmouth folk who lived through it, this grand theatre was destroyed in the big blitz. Reduced to a heap of bricks and rubble, the end of this hallowed hall, where so many aspiring performers had begun on their search for fame. I suppose it could be said, the only blessing was that this was one theatre that was not around in later years to suffer the ravages of television, or bingo halls.

The Theatre Royal

On the other side of Commercial Road, sandwiched between the White Swan Tavern and the Prudential Buildings was another entertainment palace that showed films at various times, the Theatre Royal. But once again, like the Hippodrome, theatrical productions proved to be the main attraction, and after all was what the Royal was originally intended for.

On that particular site in Commercial Road, around the mid-1800s the Landport Hall was a popular assembly place for townsfolk. But by 1856, thanks to the efforts of a Mr. Henry Rutley, it was granted a licence and converted into a theatre.

It opened in this role in September 1856, and its opening play was "A New Way To Pay Old Debts", a well tried piece featuring William Grisdale the popular tragedian. This went down well with patrons, and really set the pattern for the many successful years that this theatre enjoyed.

In the 1880s a celebrated architect of theatres named Phipps was engaged with a view to reconstructing the Theatre Royal, in fact alterations were carried out fairly regularly during the following twenty years. Another notable architect was employed for reconstruction work in 1900, this was Frank Matcham who was responsible for several of the theatres in London's West End.

The Theatre Royal was taken over by Portsmouth Theatres Ltd., a public company that was incorporated in 1897. They were happy with the success of the Royal, and had the King's Theatre in Southsea built in 1906.

But what of the artistes who graced the stage of the Theatre Royal? Those boards were trod by anybody who was anybody in the theatrical world through the years, and the list of players is far too great for us to start mentioning. But one group that could always be sure of packing them in was our very own Portsmouth Wandering Thespians, a gifted singer named Sally Bailey was a great favourite with the audiences. She later married Mr. Hoy, the editor of the Hampshire Telegraph. Another local girl who sang many times at the Royal was Evie Greene, in later years she hit the big time and became famous as a London Gaiety Girl, her picture was reproduced countless times on old postcards.

And so we skip on into the 1930s, for this is the period that interests us in our search for cinemas. The Theatre Royal became a cinema in 1932, no doubt hoping to cash in on the 'talkies' boom. The first film shown on the 7th March of that year was "Common Law", starring the beautiful Constance Bennett. Apart from odd breaks for stage productions such as pantomimes, films continued to flourish for the following sixteen years. Then in 1948 the screen was taken down, and the Theatre Royal once again reverted to live entertainment.

This theatre then went through difficult times. Despite noble efforts by a resident company led by Hector Ross, Kim Peacock and June Sylvaine in the 1950s, the end was near. It more or less closed for theatre patrons in 1959, and during the 1960s it was opened occasionally for various entertainments. All-Star Wrestling featured on this list, but it always seemed irreverent that this magnificently ornate structure should be subjected to the grunts and groans of corpulent gents attempting to dismember each other and doing it in the auditorium that was once graced by a performance from the great Russian ballet dancer Pavlova!

And so that once resplendent facia has been left to crumble and decay, but its enforced rest has by no means been a quiet one. The Theatre Royal has attracted headlines just as it once attracted audiences, and it is hoped that with the help of some dedicated folk who have the theatre's best interests at heart, it will one day enjoy some of its former glory.

The Picture House

On we go, through the Guildhall Square. Hope the lions are not roaring! Under the railway bridge and past the station, we find the cinema we are searching for. The old Picture House.

Young chaps stroll down Commercial Road, flat caps on their heads, hands in their pockets, and their lips are pursed whistling the hit song of the year "Hello! Hello! Who's Your Lady Friend?" That year is 1913, it is the 16th of December, and a large crowd is assembled at the spot known as Speedwell Buildings. The dignitaries make their speeches, and Alderman Sir George Couzens proclaims that the "Picture House" is officially open.

The Mayor of Portsmouth, Alderman J. Corke, was also present at the opening ceremony, and the proprietors announced that they would hand over the first day's box-office takings to the Mayor for a local charity of his choice. The proprietors of the Picture House were the Provincial Cinematograph Theatres Ltd. who after providing light refreshments for the dignitaries, invited them to stay and watch an excellent programme of films.

That first programme featured "The Bills of Death", coupled with "Portuguese Centaurs". The films were supported by what was described as a first-class orchestra of top musicians, and all this entertainment could be enjoyed for only sixpence, or one shilling.

It was quite a handsome building inside and out, the auditorium was reached through a marble lobby, with plenty of oak panelling interspersed with paintings depicting various scenes from naval history. It had the usual luxurious seating that every cinema of that time boasted, and the builders had also gone to great extremes to install good ventilation. They even had special filters for dispersing fog if it should find its way into the cinema.

The proprietors were also quick to point out that they had the very latest projection equipment installed, which was guaranteed free from vibration, a common fault with the showing of films around that time. This immediately conjures up a scene with the poor old projectionist desperately trying to hold the equipment down as the Waterloo train thundered over the railway bridge in Commercial Road.

It was pretty hairy at times being a projectionist, especially when the film broke down, a fairly common occurrence we might add. At such times, the audience would launch into a riotous cacophony of whistles and catcalls, plus the sound of hundreds of feet stamping in unison. This was worse in older cinemas, for the stamping would bring up clouds of dust, resulting in the audience coughing and spluttering alarmingly.

Within a few months of opening, the Picture House presented a new cinema gimmick known as "Kinetophone" - described as Edison's wonderful invention to provide talking pictures. It was presented for a short season commencing March 23rd 1914 and the posters proclaimed "Films that can be seen and heard - a playhouse, a concert hall, and a picture house all in one!" The actual films for the first show were "The Olio Minstrels", "Her Redemption" and film of the Grand National.

But I am afraid poor synchronisation caused the early demise of this particular shot at producing talking pictures, and filmgoers had to wait until the late 20s for a more perfect presentation.

We are afraid the old Picture House did not stay around long enough to witness the arrival of perfect talking pictures, it closed in the mid 20s, lay derelict for some years until 1936 when the house furnishing store of Woodhouse was built on the site. The only place of amusement in the block was Edmunds Funfair, a pleasant way to give-away pennies.

Arcade Picture Palace

We now cross Edinburgh Road, mind the trams, and stroll on to an opening by the side of Lloyds Bank. This opening was a pleasant little diversion that ran from Commercial Road back into Edinburgh Road, where Albertolli's Swiss Cafe and Restaurant stood on the corner. Oh, just to think of that wonderful establishment, where in the upstairs dining rooms you could have a sumptuous blow-out for a few bob!

But we are digressing, for we are going to the pictures. Get your cigarettes from Mr. Trewin's tobacco shop, or your sweets from Miss Emily Massey's, pay your 2d. to the nice lady in the box-office, and enter that hallowed hall known as the "Arcade Picture Palace".

The name we associate with this cinema is that of John Mills. No, Madam, not that John Mills; our John Mills owned a fair portion of The Arcade, dealing with china, carving and gilding. He did his picture framing from a workshop in Fountain Street. Anyway, he was proprietor of the Arcade Cinema, next to Mills bookshop and stationers.

The Arcade Picture Palace began life in 1910, it enjoyed a steady patronage in its early years, for the filmgoers were anxious to view footage of topical events, and there was certainly plenty of those to see. Those events had a very royal flavour, with the death of Edward the Seventh in 1910, and the coronation of George the Fifth in 1911, plus the investiture of the Prince of Wales at Caernarvon Castle.

Business was good for the Arcade Cinema, so in 1913 it underwent alterations and some rebuilding. This resulted in more comfortable seats for the patrons, of whom it could hold 500, still at popular prices, and we do mean popular! 2d., 3d. and 4d. Matinees were held daily from 2.30 to 4.30pm and the evening performances were from 6 to 10.30pm.

Children had their own special matinees on Saturdays, and if

The "Arcade Cinema"

you could not creep in hidden under someones rain coat, or bunk it through the toilet window, you had to pay the sum of one penny for this privilege! But what the heck, it must be worth a penny to see the deadpan features of William S. Hart hardly move a muscle as the baddies try to part him from his best pal, which more often than not was his old nag. No Madam, his horse, not his wife!

Our old friend Bill Bonwick was also associated with the Arcade Cinema, never one to be shy and retiring, he was always to the fore with topical programme advertising. But when you got down to it, it was still on the same theme as the other cinemas. They always showed clear and steady pictures, and they always had the best orchestra in town! In the case of the Arcade, the orchestra was under the direction of Harry Williams, who enjoyed a good following with his jazz band.

It is worth noting that in 1920 those popular prices went up alarmingly! To 6d., 9d., 1/- and 1/6d.!

The Arcade Cinema did survive into the talking film age, and indeed held its facia high despite the increasing number of more de-luxe picture houses that came into existence in the pre-war years. But I am afraid one competitor it could not survive was a bomb, and like so many others it was destroyed on that dreaded date of January 10th in 1941.

Only a few days before, on January 6th, the Portsmouth Branch of the Cinematograph Exhibitors Association had announced that all cinemas in the City of Portsmouth could remain open until 10pm., instead of 9pm. Well, Mister Hitler made sure the Arcade Cinema did not open again. The last films shown were "Dr. Syn" and "It's All Yours". So ended the life of another popular Portsmouth establishment.

The Classic

Many readers will have memories of trips to London on which, if you had an hour to spare, you could shelter in one of those intimate little news theatres that appeared to abound there. Apart from catching up with the latest film news, you could also chortle at the escapades of Mickey Mouse or Donald Duck, or maybe have mild hysterics at the antics of the Three Stooges.

It was unusual to find cinemas of this type outside London, and it is interesting to recall that one of the first to open in the provinces was in Portsmouth. It was sited in Commercial Road, sandwiched between the Home & Colonial Stores and Dunns, the hatters, and opened as the 'Cinenews'. This haven for Walt Disney fans began its film screening life on the 14th of September in 1936.

The price of admission was 6d. and 1/- and the filmfare was news, cartoons and interest. The cinema was designed for 'Capitol and Provincial News Theatres Ltd.' by Allister MacDonald, the talented architect son of the former Prime Minister, Ramsey MacDonald. The screen was slightly tilted so as to eliminate eye-strain, and the sound system was as good as could be heard anywhere in the country.

In 1937 the Cinenews was renamed 'The Classic', and the fact was marked with the showing of "David Copperfield" on July the 5th. Movie buffs will have fond memories of this classic with the bulbous-nosed W.C. Fields and the angelic Freddie Bartholomew.

That was the first of many great films the Classic was to show in the following thirty years, always striving to present good entertainment. Towards the latter end of its life, it was one of the first cinemas in the area to show late-night movies - usually films in the horror mode. One has to possess great stamina to attend these shows, no matter how gripping the movie, there is always the tendency to doze off! Then you are liable to receive a rude awakening, usually from the "Monster from 20,000 Fathoms" raising its ugly head out of the screen towards your seat! The other off-putting thing with late-night films is the tramplike gents who always manage to sit next to you, they also snooze off and you find they lay their heads on your shoulder through the rest of the programme!

The Classic closed its doors for day and night filmgoers in August of 1972, the last film shown was "The Cruel Sea". The site reverted to a shop, and Portsmouth had lost another name on its list of weekly entertainments.

Keast's Gaiety Picture Palace

Now 1912 was a strange year, with plenty of ups and downs. One of the downs was the sinking of the Titanic, but one of the ups was that you could visit the Gaiety Picture Palace in Commercial Road. It was built by John Lay & Co. for one of the greatest showmen to grace the fair city of Portsmouth, a larger than life character known as William Keast.

Keast's lifestyle was probably more exciting than many of the films that were shown at the Gaiety, at one time he had taken part in the great Klondyke gold-rush, so you can be sure he was a pretty tough customer.

The most patrons this cinema could hold was around 150, and they were seated on hard wooden benches. Although the films were silent, the projector certainly was not, it made the most awful noise you could imagine. The only thing that the Gaiety really had in its favour was that it was one of the first cinemas in the area with a sloping floor, although another plus was that the admission charges were only 1d. and 2d. An added bonus being that if you cut a coupon out of the newspaper you could have a 2d. seat for 1d.

The Gaiety Picture Palace closed down towards the end of the First World War, and the site was later taken over by Messrs. David Grieg, the grocers.

The Savoy (A.B.C.)

Strolling past the Suffolk Arms on the corner of Providence Path, past many little shops that catered for the needs of the area, past the gates of the Royal Hospital, on the corner of Fitzherbert Street in 1937 we would have found the Savoy Cinema. In fact it is still to be found there, going under the abbreviated title of the A.B.C.

The year 1937 may be best remembered by some filmgoers for the showing of "Ecstasy", in which the delectable Heddy Lamarr bared her all in a nude swimming sequence. But the film patrons of Portsmouth will remember it for the opening of the Savoy, one of the most luxurious cinemas outside the West End.

That opening took place on Saturday the 17th of July, with the Lord and Lady Mayoress lending their presence. All the seats in the stalls were 6d., and all the circle seats were 1/-. For that sum the first-nighters saw "That Girl From Paris", starring Jack Oakie, Lily Ponds and heart-throb Gene Raymond. Whilst appearing live from the depths of the Savoy we had that fine organist, Reginald Porter Brown, passing his educated feet over the pedals of the Compton Wonder Organ.

During the 12 months prior to 1937, five cinemas were built in the city of Portsmouth, the Savoy being the fifth. The aim in that particular period was to make going to the pictures something special and the Savoy certainly imparted that feeling. As one enters even the paybox is different with a bridge over leading to a balcony from which one reaches a well furnished lounge. Concealed lighting, deep carpets, telephones, comfortable seating. Yes, it was certainly more comfy than most of the lounges we had to go home to.

Not a lot more can be said about this particular cinema, as the A.B.C. it has remained one of Portsmouth's premier cinemas, showing top films and still supplying the same luxurious trappings. Although we accept luxury more easily nowadays.

This cinema brings to an end our stroll through the past and present cinemas of Commercial Road. There were others, but as most of them opened and closed within the first year, we feel them hardly worthy of mention.

Take a deep breath, rest your feet for a moment, and then we will be on our way to view more Portsmouth dream palaces.

The Paragon Picture Palace

Strolling back down Commercial Road, we return to the Gaiety. Then if we cross the road we will find Lake Road, and that is where we shall continue our journey. Now the strange fact about entertainment places in this road appears to be that their titles more often than not began with the letter 'P'.

One such place with the intended title of 'The Pavilion', we shall dismiss straight away. It was intended to open it in 1913, but a licence was never granted owing to the building being deemed unsuitable by the authorities. So it's hail and farewell to the Pavilion.

But still harping on the initial 'P', Lake Road most certainly did have a cinema named 'The Paragon' and this establishment did enjoy use for a number of years. In fact, it dealt out its weekly dose of film fun for about seventeen years, beginning life around 1910. But it disappeared about 1927. That is for cinema purposes, but we believe it later emerged as the Paragon Temperance Billiard Hall. Temperance being the operative word, for it was sited next to the Salvation Army Barracks.

The Strand

Moving up Lake Road, just before we got to the Shannon public house, we find the 'Strand Kinema'. This cinema was built for a Mr. Martin by Mr. F. Corke, the architects being Messrs. Smith and Smith. It opened its doors on the 11th of April 1914.

It was fairly comfortable for cinemas of that period, with tip-up seats for which the patrons paid 2d., 3d. and 4d. And like the others it was not shy in proclaiming the musical ability of its orchestra, which consisted of six chaps blowing, scraping and thumping away like crazy! And as if this were not enough, by 1918 a pipe organ weighing two tons was installed. It was claimed that this was equal to an orchestra of fifty! Wow, pass the earplugs!

Of course, prices had shot up like mad by 1921: 4d., 5d. and 8d. Ridiculous! Who would pay 8d. to go to the pictures? Also that year, the films were billed as being shown by means of "Martin's Famous Screen Light", which we can only assume was some gimmick thought up by the proprietor, Mr. Martin.

Anyway, the Strand stayed in business long enough to exhibit the first 'talkie', and our old friend Al (You ain't heard nothin' yet) Jolson, did his stuff in "The Jazz Singer" in May 1929.

But the end was near, the Strand was closed in april 1930, and the last film was "The Time, The Place, and The Girl". That was the bad news, but the good news was that it opened again on Wednesday the 21st of May in 1930 as the "Strand Roller Skating Rink", fitted with the very latest maple floor. Ouch!

By the war years the building became Phillips Furniture Store, and then once again on the dreaded January 10th 1941, bombs destroyed the establishment we once knew as the Strand. This can only bring one to the conclusion that Mister Hitler could not have been a great film fan - he closed more cinemas than Bingo!

The Princes

Walking past the Shannon, not forgetting to say "Good Morning" to Mr. Hagen, the landlord, we find the Baptist Church. Now this was rather strange, for this place of worship was sandwiched between two pubs and one theatre. The two pubs being the afore-mentioned Shannon, and the Sultan on the corner of Alexandra Road. The theatre was named 'The Princes'.

The Princes first opened in Lake Road in the 1860s as a circus but this did not go down too well, so it changed into a theatre. Presenting plays mostly, but at times delving into the realms of music-hall, the theatre had varying degrees of popularity, but a mass of interesting stories.

Before we start plastering on the old grease paint, and go leaping into our Henry Irving "The Bells" bit, we have to show great control and remind ourselves that we are dealing with cinemas.

As far as the Princes is concerned, its film career started in 1924. It was bought from Portsmouth Theatres Limited by Messrs. Davidson and Zeid, who spared no expense to convert it into a de-luxe picture house. It had a seating capacity of 1,650, and so could rightly be claimed at that time to be one of the largest places of amusement in Portsmouth.

The first film was shown on Boxing Day of that year. it was "Down To The Sea In Ships", starring the 'It' girl herself, the wide-eyed Clara Bow. As usual many local dignitaries were on hand for the opening, although Mayor Frank Privett could not attend owing to illness. Bearing the film in mind, perhaps he suffered from sea-sickness. Anyway, enough people turned up for that first night, every seat was taken and many people were turned away.

After the happy patrons had piled out of the Princes, a select band proceeded to lash into a super supper on the stage, laid on by Mr. Zeid. Those interested were shown the projection box, where they could inspect the equipment, which of course was the most up-to-date that money could buy.

Through the pre-war years the Princes packed them in, and many older residents of Portsmouth will have happy memories of hours spent in the darkness of this cinema. The films were not bad either!

But I am afraid this cinema did not even survive until January 1941. On August the 24th 1940 the bombs did their worst and that was the end of the Princes. For movie buffs, the last films shown were "The Gates of Alcatraz" and "Bulldog Drummond at Bay". This Bulldog Drummond starred John Lodge for a change, not Ronald Colman or Jack Buchanan.

The People's Palace - The Palladium

To find our last cinema in Lake Road we continue in the Kingston Road direction, past Drummond Road and up to the corner of Leonard Road. On this site many readers will recall 'The Palladium' of pre-war years; but this place of entertainment originally enjoyed the title of 'The People's Palace'.

It started life in the 1880s as a Temperance Music Hall. To explain the title it simply meant that there were no ladies of dubious pleasure or drinks available. A quite unusual departure for music halls in those days. It was built by Frank and Bob Pearce, and Frank and his wife, Harriet, ran the hall. They were both staunch temperance workers needless to say.

And so the stage of the People's Palace resounded to the sounds of a 'Smile, a Joke and a Song', for the hall was let to a great showbiz character by the name of Harry Vento. As the name will readily explain, Harry was a ventriloquist. Before the 1900s this type of "Gottle of Geer" act was fairly unusual, hence the reasonable success of "Vento's Music Hall".

It is almost possible to write a book on the exploits of Vento alone but we must move on to the subject in hand. In 1891 the Portsmouth magistrates would not grant a licence owing to the bad state of the building, Frank Pearce blamed Vento for this state of affairs and eventually re-possessed the building. Frank and his good lady, Harriet, soon got the structure back into shape, and by 1892 the licence had been granted and music hall reigned once again at the People's Palace.

Many great artistes from the past appeared on the Lake Road stage, amongst them was the previously mentioned, Vesta Tilley, moonlighting from the Hippodrome. Another popular lady was Hetty King, who always went down well in Portsmouth, especially with her "All the nice girls love a sailor".

But we are putting on our grease-paint again, are we not? In October 1904 the People's Palace advertised "Le Clairs

People's Palace, Lake Road, Portsmouth

Animated Pictures'', so venturing into the world of moving pictures. We may add that the pictures were supported by variety acts.

Frank Pearce retired from the entertainment world, and by 1920 the People's Palace was renamed 'The Palladium', and the showing of films was the name of the game. And yet once again, Boxing Day was the opening date of this cinema, the first film being "Sins of the Children" with a good supporting programme of shorts and comedies. Fifty per cent of the first day's takings were donated to charity, namely the Goodwill Fund.

The Palladium just about reached the 'talkies' age, but with its proprietors the 'Cosham Picture House Limited' going into liquidation in the early 30s, the doors of the Palladium closed in November 1930. Several re-openings were proposed but they

never transpired. No sight is sadder than that of a derelict cinema; the Palladium suffered this fate until it was used as a warehouse for Messrs. Blundells in later years. It has now disappeared completely, no sign of the entertainment palace that gave so much pleasure in its day, lost along with the artistes that once trod its boards.

Fratton Electric Theatre
And as we say farewell to Lake Road, we start on a new thoroughfare, in which we shall be having a look at no less than eight cinemas in one stretch. But we shall have to walk down to Fratton Bridge to start our jaunt first.

There we are, that didn't take long did it? Just around the corner in 1910 we would have seen the 'Fratton Electric', in fact it opened on the 30th of July of that year. The theatre was finished in an exceptionally handsome style: it was a rather high and roomy building that could accommodate 250 persons, sitting of course yet once again in richly upholstered seats, the height of luxury.

Under the auspices of the Fratton Electric Theatre Company, the cinema had been fitted throughout with electric light, and vows were made that they would provide the best and latest in animated pictures. On that first day the patrons paid 3d. for front seats or 6d. for back. The first film they saw was "A Champion Boxer" coupled with "Girl on the Triple 'X' Ranch".

In the early days of this Fratton cinema, matinees were presented on Wednesdays and Saturdays. It is interesting to note that for these afternoon performances, tea was provided for the patrons.

But I am afraid the Fratton Electric Theatre did not enjoy a long life, the entrance doors were closed during the early part of 1918, and the site is now used as a club by the British Legion.

"Fratton Electric"
Now British Legion

The Bijou

Strolling down Fratton Road to where the Co-operative emporium now stands, we would have found Dorset Street in days gone by. On that corner was the old 'Bijou' cinema, long since gone. That is a marvellous name to give a picture house, and I am afraid there cannot be many places left, if any, still functioning with that name.

In the dictionary the word 'Bijou' means Jewel, Small and Elegant. Well, the Fratton Bijou was certainly that, it only had 260 seats. It opened for business in 1910, and was built for a Mr. H. White. But it did in fact change hands several times, in a very short space of time we might add, for the Bijou closed in 1917. So that was the end of another cinema where Charlie Chaplin would never grace the screen again.

The Troxy

Would you like some good news? The next picture house is not far away! Now that really was good news a few years ago when cinemas were not so far apart for we addicts would come straight out of one and into another.

Shielding our eyes against the bright daylight, one of the cinemas we might have staggered into was the 'Troxy'. That is if the lure of the demon drink was not stronger - for the 'Dog and Duck' is on one side and the 'Guardsman' on the other.

The Troxy opened its doors in 1936 on the 30th of July, its proprietors being Tivoli Ltd. This was a magnificent building for its day, catering for 2,000 patrons who were happy to pay 6d. for a seat downstairs, or for those with aspirations to reach the heights, a balcony seat could be purchased for 1/-.

The first film shown was "Queen of Hearts" starring the one and only Gracie Fields, who was at the peak of her fame during that period. But of course 1936 was a great year for films. Take your pick: "Rose Marie" with Jeanette MacDonald and Nelson Eddy, "Camille" with Greta Garbo, "Showboat" with Allan

Jones and Irene Dunne, Gary Cooper in "The Plainsman". The list goes on and on!

The Troxy showed its fair share of these gems until 1941 during the war years - for then it was used as a food store. This was a bit of a comedown for a building that cost £50,000 but at least it did not get bombed. It re-opened in 1946 on the 30th of September and the film shown was "Anchors Aweigh", which you may recall had Gene Kelly and Frank Sinatra romping around in silly sailor suits.

In flocked the customers for the following twenty years or so. One of the Troxy's brighter moments in that time was in 1954 - they were the first cinema in Portsmouth to show a film in Cinemascope. This of course was "The Robe" with Burton and Mature.

Then I am afraid the Troxy suffered the fate of so many of its type: it became a Bingo Hall. In fact, it still is.

The Globe - The Rex

Carrying on from the Troxy up Fratton Road, past Arundel Street, before we reach the Carnegie Free Library, and there it is: 'The Globe'. Or at least it was, for this cinema changed names several times. It opened as the Globe on the 19th of December in 1913 and the first programme was "Convict 482" and "Those Who Live In Glass Houses". The price of admission was 3d., 6d. and 9d. and it was open 6-10.30pm.

The first change in name came in 1937, taken over by Tivoli (Portsmouth) Ltd., the Globe became 'The Rex'. This is the name that will be more familiar to readers. Under the new name it was tarted up considerably. It was even given a false ceiling. It could accommodate 410 patrons downstairs and 90 in the Upper Circle. The very latest in equipment was installed, so it was all systems go.

And it certainly started with a good rabble-rouser on May 24th 1937 with "Captain Blood", this was the first film that the King of the Swashbucklers, Errol Flynn, made, so beginning his epic fencing duels with the King of the Nasties, Basil Rathbone.

The proprietors adopted a deliberate policy of showing for a second time famous films that may have been missed the first time around, dismissing the fact that the filmgoer may have wanted to miss them first time around!

Along came the war and like the Troxy, the Rex closed its doors and became a storehouse. But it re-opened in the July of 1945 with "Jitterbugs" and "Stormy Weather". "Jitterbugs" starred our old friends Laurel and Hardy, and what better filmfare to open a cinema with.

The Rex closed on the 4th of March 1950 but re-opened a couple of weeks later under its new name of 'Rex Continental' by showing "Rome - Open City". My word, what would Laurel and Hardy have said!

But even that name changed in April 1972. It became the 'Curzon Cinema Club', for members only. If we state that the first film shown under this banner was "The Sexy Adventures of the Three Musketeers" coupled with "Bang-bang", we feel this tells it all!

Then a few months later, in October 1972, guess what happened? Yes, that's right - the name changed again! It was now the 'Classic International Film Theatre', one of the Classic Cinemas chain. The first film shown on October 20th was "Investigation of a Citizen Above Suspicion", an Italian piece with English subtitles. We find foreign films are okay, but find it hard to adjust to the sight of Brigitte Bardot with words on the bottom. The film's bottom, not Brigitte's!

This Fratton Road cinema was by now fitted out in a more intimate style, the accent being on comfort set in a modern decor, and fully carpeted. All of which was a far cry from the old 'Fleapit' image of times gone by.

Undergoing another name change in 1973, it became known as the 'Tatler', for members only. Bringing us up to date, it has reverted to 'The Classic' and is at present screening some of the best popular films that are available.

The Shaftesbury

Keeping on the same stretch of road, and pointing our weary feet still to the north, we leave Fratton Road and merge into Kingston Road. Walking past New Road, on the same side we are getting near our objective. No Madam, not Voller's Corset Emporium. We are referring to the old 'Shaftesbury Hall'!

This name will bring memories flooding back to older readers, and not many of them may realise that this site was formerly that of a chapel. But in 1910 the building was re-designed and emerged as the Shaftesbury Hall. Around £8,000 was spent on this work and the result was handsome. A fine example of Edwardian architecture. The coup-de-grace as it were being the statue of Mercury proudly sitting atop the building.

The first manager, Herbert Cole, was very pleased with the response of the public to the first programme. This included the screen showing of the "Last Days of Pompeii", whilst on the stage two songs were sung by Miss Dorothy Alexander and Mr. Henry Cook gave what was described as an interesting recitation. We may add the excellent orchestra was under the direction of Mr. C. Gann. This was in the days before the great organ was installed.

As you can imagine, this was a complete transformation for the site that had once been the old Buckland Congregational Church, but the Shaftesbury, through the years, attracted its own brand of worshippers. This was largely due to the efforts of Henry Cook, helped by his sister Miss V. Cook. Henry had gained plenty of cinema experience with travelling film shows in the pre-1910 days. One of the most popular singers to grace the stage of the Shaftesbury between films was Winifred Dore, and her rendering

Shaftesbury Hall, (with statue)
Kingston Road, Portsmouth

of "The Lost Chord" was guaranteed to leave not a dry eye in the house.

During the Second World War the stores adjacent to the Shaftesbury were gutted in an air-raid but the cinema was unharmed. However, some years later a bit of burst shell was found on the premises, and strangely enough this piece of shrapnel was formed in the shape of Winston Churchill's famous 'V' sign!

The cinema closed in 1959 and became a Bingo Hall. However, in 1969 the balcony was converted into a small cinema and opened as 'The Tatler'. This changed in 1973 to 'The Vogue' and even more changes were to follow: 'The Classic' and 'The Mecca'.

But it closed in 1975 as a cinema and bingo took over. So when the cry goes up of "Full house", it would not be surprising to learn that the face beamed of dear old Henry Cook in Heaven. But of course it is not the kind of full house he looked forward to.

Majestic

On the other side of the road going towards Kingston Cross, we find 'The Majestic'. Like the Shaftesbury this cinema also was built in the classical style, under the personal supervision of the proprietor, Richard Stokes.

Mr. Stokes was the 'Guvnor' and what he said went. He spent £50,000 on the building of his Majestic and believed in getting good value for money. This picture house opened in 1921 on December 5th with "A Yankee in the Court of King Arthur". This of course was the silent version, a talking version was made in later years: a romp for Bing Crosby, William Bandix and Cedric Hardwicke.

As well as being a good looking building, it had a very strong construction. There were four great pillars adjoining the screen and the plaster work of the ceiling lent a rather oriental touch to the auditorium.

The Majestic also had a very talented orchestra, patrons coming to listen to its musical arrangements regardless of the showing of films. The orchestra leader was Austin Beech and he was naturally redundant with the coming of the 'talkies'. Although the Guvnor was hard, he looked after his staff and made Mr. Beech a doorman instead.

It was very much a one-man cinema, ruled over by Mr. Stokes until his death in 1934 at the age of 74. He did at least see it through the start of the 'talkies', the first of which to be shown at the Majestic was "Melody of Love" with Walter Pigeon and Mildred Harris.

In 1951 the cinema was faced with having to increase its safety precautions. This meant having to acquire neighbouring properties, a great expense. And so the Majestic was sold to the Essoldo chain. In later years it became 'The Classic' but it closed as a cinema in 1973. After extensive alterations, it re-opened in 1976 as the Portsmouth Billiard and Snooker Club. I suppose you could say that the Majestic went to 'pot'!

Majestic, Kingston Road

Regent - Gaumont

Still carrying on in a straight line, we flow into London Road, North End. On the left hand side was the resplendent 'Regent Cinema' and in 1923 the people of Portsmouth saw the glory of what was once Rome. Well, Greece anyway. For the London architect, Mr. S. Clough, endeavoured with this building to carry

Gaumont, London Road, North End - 1953

Gaumont, North End
Foyer

the cinema patrons right away from their orthodox surroundings via Grecian decor, with plenty of pillars on view.

It really was lavish, the ceiling was like a sky of blue with the sun's rays coming across the auditorium, produced by clever lighting. As the lights dimmed the presence of moonlight was suggested with twinkling stars overhead. One was liable to forget that one had actually come to the Regent to see a film.

The film the patrons had come to see on opening day, the 31st of March 1923, was Jackie Coogan in "Oliver Twist". Coogan had sprung to fame in "The Kid" with Chaplin a few years earlier. The next presentation on April the 2nd was Rudolph Valentino in "Blood and Sand" and that really packed in the

Stage of Gaumont, North End

GAUMONT
BOYS' AND GIRLS' CLUB

President: J. ARTHUR RANK, J.P.

RULES

Club meetings are held every Saturday morning.

Members agree to abide by the rules of the Committee and at all times to obey Club Chief.

Club badges must be worn at all performances.

Advert

2,500 patrons that the Regent could hold. Seats were of course available at popular prices - well they were popular with the management anyway! The cheapest seat was 6d. and the dearest was 2/-. What, 2/- to go to the pictures! Who could afford that?

The Regent opened under the auspices of the Palace Picture House (Portsmouth) Ltd. By 1928 the Regent Orchestra was boasted as being the finest on the South Coast. It was under the direction of Sidney Shinebourne, late of the Queen's Orchestra from London, and a great violinist. Some patrons attended two nights running, just to listen to the thirty melodious minutes allocated to the orchestra for their solo spot.

The Regent survived the war pretty well, and the onslaught of film fans who flocked to the cinema after the war. These were the sunshine days of the cinema, when folk did not mind waiting for hours outside just to see a film. And these were also the days when the British people still expressed their feelings during visits to the pictures - a sort of hangover from the war. It was noted in 1951 during a newsreel at the Regent, that when Winston Churchill appeared on the screen the audience broke into thunderous applause, but when poor old Clem Attlee came on there was stony silence!

Not only was there a change of government around that period, the Regent underwent a change of name also, it became the Gaumont. Under that banner it continued to entertain the masses for twenty years or so, but by the early 70s those masses were getting depleted. The doors closed, and this magnificent building was demolished in 1974. So ended the half century run of one of Portsmouth's most luxurious cinemas.

The Odeon

But still moving northwards on the other side of the road, there is still a cinema operating, in fact three cinemas. All will be revealed a few paragraphs on.

On the night of December 14th 1936, North End witnessed the opening of another cinema in the vast Odeon chain. The Lord Mayor Councillor F. Spickernell turned up to perform the ceremony, accompanied by the Band of the Royal Marines, with Lt. V. Dunn conducting. The audience sat spellbound in their 2,000 luxurious seats.

The Odeon's opening film was "Chick", starring Sydney Howard. Do you remember dear old Sydney Howard? Rotten, wasn't he!

This cinema survived the war bombings, and also continued after the war exhibiting good filmfare. The momentous happening in the history of the Odeon at North End was in 1973, it was made into a triple cinema. This really was good thinking, three mini-cinemas under one roof, catering for different tastes. Anyway, on August 26th that year it presented: "A Touch of Class" on Screen One, "Live and Let Die" on Screen Two and "Godspell" on Screen Three. See what we mean by catering for all tastes!

The marvellous thing is it appears to have worked, for the Odeon Film Centre is still flourishing in 1981. This is great for the film industry and great for the fans.

Odeon, North End

North End Cinerama - Empire - Forum

To visit our next cinema of cinematic delight, we will have to cut through the back streets of Stamshaw. There it is, right on the corner of Wilson Road. Most readers will be familiar with the 'Forum' but did you know it had a few other names before that? No sir, not those sort of names!

A crowd waits on that corner on a cold December day in 1912. It was in fact two days before Christmas. What are they doing here? Surely they should be heading towards Charlotte Street to get their Xmas bird. The doors open, and they pile into the building that has the words 'North End Cinerama' proudly displayed outside.

It was billed as comparing in comfort with any picture house and the publicity blurb went to great lengths to tell us that this entertainment palace was the enterprise of Mr. Sprigings, a gentleman prominently connnected with the area. And we are pleased to know that he made sure the prices charged would suit a very large prospective clientele. The admission charge was in fact 3d., 6d. and 9d. for balcony seats.

By 1926 the name was changed to 'The Empire' but in 1938 the cinema was closed to undergo great alterations. Of course one of those alterations just had to be the name: hence 'The Forum'. And what a marvellous programme they presented for the opening: Glenn Morris in "Tarzan's Revenge", coupled with the film favourite of all time, Will Hay, in "Oh, Mr. Porter".

That was the programme for the Forum's opening on the 8th September 1938 and you may wish to know the programme for its closing, for this sad happening did occur on the 28th February 1959. The films were "Private's Progress" and "The Baby and the Battleship". The building was turned into a store. Let us have a minute's silence for the dear old Forum.

Empire - later Forum - Stamshaw Road, North End

The Copnor Electric

Now I am afraid we have got to make a bit of a journey across town so just pick your year and your transport accordingly. Trams, buses, car or even pushbike. No matter how you get there, just get there. For the next picture house on the agenda is well worth the effort. Good, glad you made it. We are now standing in Copnor Road, in between Powerscourt Road and Chichester Road. Now look up and read the sign, 'Copnor Electric Theatre'.

The story of this cinema begins in 1911, for in that year on July 19th proprietor Mr. Langdown opened the doors to an eager public. Offering the latest attractions, the publicity proclaimed that the ventilation was excellent; it had three large exits affording peace of mind; and the scent spraying is grateful. All we

New Forum, Stamshaw Road - 1938
Ex-Empire

can say is that the scent must have been a different brand to the type usually employed, that smelt more like 'Evening in Charlotte Street'.

The first films shown were "The Squatter's Daughter", coupled with "Insurrecto" and plenty of supporting shorts. The licence changed hands several times during the Copnor Electric's life, almost once a year.

Old Portsmouth resident, Harry Camfield has fond memories of the Copnor Electric. In the 20s he remembers a family outing to this picture house to celebrate his grandfather's 90th birthday. The old chap was absolutely enthralled with the visit and could not stop talking about the antics of Charlie Chaplin. Grandad had been a violinist at the King's Theatre for many years, and when the family got home from the pictures he produced his violin and knocked out a tune even though his hands were badly bent with arthritis.

A not so happy event happened at the Copnor Electric in 1928. One of the staff opened the door of the projection box to find projectionist Albert Morgan with a rope round his neck, hanging from the ceiling. It was stated later that Albert was in a very depressed state, evidently because his girlfriend's mother had bullied him!

The Copnor Electric closed in the following year - it was November 1929. But that was not quite the end, part of the building was used for another cinema. Read on.

The Tivoli

The 'Tivoli Cinema' opened on Boxing Day 1929; it was built on the site of the Copnor Electric Cinema, in fact the entrance, queue room and principal cloakroom was adapted from the old cinema. If you were not lucky enough to be able to get into the queue room, you had to wait outside, and the exterior was finished in a white cement to depict a Spanish style with an open colonnade at the front.

The entrance lounge was 70ft. long by 25ft. wide and you paid your admission fee, 6d to 1/3d. at a pay desk in the centre. The auditorium was also quite large for those days, this was also in Spanish style, and the ceiling gave an open-air night effect, stars included.

A Western Electric Sound System was installed in the Tivoli. The 'talkies' were upon us and even at a cost of £4,000 for the installation, cinemas were redundant without a sound system. The first film shown was "Why Leave Home" starring Nick Stuart and Sue Carol, two actors of whom Cecil B. De Mille once said "Who?".

Like others of its kind, the Tivoli closed during the war and was

Tivoli, Copnor Road, Portsmouth

Eagledrome, New Road - 1911

used as a store for food and furniture. It opened after the war, but we are afraid the writing was on the wall, Spanish wall of course. The Tivoli closed to make way for a garage and petrol station.

The Eagle Picturedrome

Our old friend Harry Camfield from the Copnor Electric story also remembers going to the pictures in New Road, opposite the Kingston Cemetary. This was the 'Eagle Picturedrome', an establishment opened in August 1911 by Mr. T. White. As usual the handbills boasted of the luxury and comfort of the building and how they intended to present the best entertainment that money could buy.

They certainly gave good value with the first programmes, in fact one of these had no less than five films. Mind you, they

probably only lasted ten minutes each. One of them in September 1911 had the intrigueing title of "Who Is Nellie?" and it was coupled with "Tontolini Shooting", which sounds rather like a spaghetti western version of the "Lone Ranger".

The Eagle Picturedrome did not enjoy an exceptionally long life, in fact it was closed by the 1920s, the site being taken over completely by Ward's Bakery.

The Grand Kinema

We are now back to Fratton. On reaching Arundel Street, down we go, for this street contained at least two cinemas we must not miss.

Getting near to the Commercial Road end we look for Upper Arundel Street, and that is where over 50 years ago we would have found 'The Grand Kinema'. This cinema was quite unique for the fact that instead of opening on a Boxing Day, it opened on an August Bank Holiday. In 1911 to be exact. Under the proprietorship of the Landport Electric Theatre Limited, this cinema could accommodate 600 patrons.

The first films shown on the 2nd of August were "The Penalty", "Jim, the Mule Boy", "Woman Without A Heart" and plenty of shorts. Price of admission: 2d., 3d. and 6d.

The Grand hardly got into the 'talkie' age. It closed at the end of 1930, the last film screened being "Dame Chance" on the 6th of December. It was not long before the site was taken over for religious purposes, namely the Elim Tabernacle.

The Trafalgar - The Rialto

The next cinema is not very far away, in fact on the same side not far from Landports Drapery Bazaar. And for a place such as Portsmouth, what better than a cinema named 'The Trafalgar'. In fact when the Trafalgar was opened in 1924, H.M.S. Victory was being fitted out for the tourists of the future. She was put into dry berth in 1922 and opened for business in 1928.

The Trafalgar Kinema certainly had a nautical flavour, as you went in the pay-box was ornamented by a ship's steering wheel, above which was a miniature of the anchor of H.M.S. Victory, whilst below there were two small lifebouys inscribed "Trafalgar".

This cinema was erected by Mr. Pounds, and some of the bricks and materials used in the construction were from the old St. Mary's Church in Gunwharf Road. Pillars were depicted as torpedo tubes, they were in fact four air tubes removed from a diving bell that was used in the construction of the concrete base of the 240 ton cantilever crane in the Dockyard.

Opening on the 24th of March in 1924, the first films shown were "A Chapter in Her Life" and "Living Lies". The manage-ment were also quick to point out that the operating room had the very latest Gaumont projector installed.

But in 1929 this 900 seater picture house was re-decorated throughout and living up to the showbiz adage of "Keep them guessing", it had a change of name.

The Rialto

And so the old Trafalgar was greatly tarted up and under its new name of 'Rialto' on the 3rd of December 1929, it presented "Some Mother's Boy", supported by "The Hit of the Show".

It was also fitted with new equipment, allowing the Rialto to present talking pictures a month later in the early part of 1930. It is interesting that in March of that year, this cinema screened a film named simply "Terrors". This picture was actually made in Portsmouth, at studios in Kingston Crescent. It was made by Mr. Osborne-Smith, of waxworks fame in the Isle of Wight and included local Portsmouth folk acting in it. Three of these were the Cheer Boys. "Terrors" was a silent film but nevertheless it was acclaimed as Osborne-Smith's best picture. In fact excerpts were shown from it on television in "The Bioscope Days" in recent years.

So the Rialto continued merrily on in the pre-war years, becoming one of Portsmouth's most popular cinemas. And then on that fated night of January 10th once again, bombs fell on the Rialto, making 1941 its closing year. The last films shown were George Formby in "Off the Dole" and Bob Hope in "Give Me a Sailor".

The Queens Cinema

We will now continue past Landport's Drapery Bazaar, cut into Edinburgh Road and carry on until we come to Queen Street. Near the corner of Hay Street was a cinema that will bring back happy memories to older residents of that area, need we tell that it was the 'Queen's Cinema?

At one time this cinema had two well known Portsmouth firms of photographers either side of it; these being Abrahams and Cozens. George Marsh's stationers shop was also in the block, doubling as a sub-post office.

The Queens started in 1914, it had formerly been Cavenders Snuff and Tobacco factory. It could seat around 550 people, including the balcony. This cinema had a rather unhappy existence and changed hands several times. In the silent days they even had a job to get pianists to accompany the films, for most of them were ladies and their fathers would not let them play at the Queens because the area had such a bad reputation in those days, especially after dark.

Box-office takings were pretty poor in the early 30s at the Queens and this led to Mr. Guy, the projectionist, entering the main office on the 6th of April 1931 and finding that the proprietor, Mr. Bingham, had shot himself in the head. The body of this poor unfortunate man was removed to the mortuary and the Queens was closed.

It re-opened later in the year with 'talkies' and the name was embelished to 'The New Queens Cinema' but it still continued to change hands frequently. This picture house survived the war, although it had some narrow escapes as one can imagine, being so close to the Dockyard. It also survived the post-war years for a while, but it could not compete with the super, more luxurious cinemas and its doors closed for good. Never really a happy picture house, for proprietors anyway.

The Plaza

The year 1928 was an outstanding one for filmgoers in the Bradford Junction area of Southsea, for that was the year that the 'Plaza' opened. Built at a time when it was realised that cinemas were here to stay, or so we thought, the Plaza was a magnificent structure. Designed by local architects Henry Dyer and Sons,

Gaumont, Bradford Junction
Ex-Plaza

once again it had the open-air theme, even to the point of cloud effects. On the right of the auditorium the audience looked through an open collonade at a scene of the Grand Canal in Venice, whilst on the left they had the view of an Italian garden, the whole being enhanced by clever lighting.

The entrance hall was designed in Tudor style, with fireplaces and sunken carpets. It also had a very large queue space where an entire audience could wait under cover, and the balcony had its own waiting area, decorated and furnished in the Adam style.

With this luxurious appearance the Plaza opened with a one-night special show on Saturday 29th September. The proprietor, Mr. Spickernell welcomed Councillor Privett, the Lord Mayor, and the Lady Mayoress. After much patting on the back, the ensemble settled down to watch "Baby Mine" and "The Elephant's Elbows". Of one fact there was no doubt, everyone was full of praise for the fine Plaza orchestra, delighting in a programme of classical and syncopated music.

After the Sunday, day of rest, the cinema opened in full earnest for the public on Monday the 1st of October, showing the marvellous "Garden of Allah", this of course being the silent version.

And so everyone was happy. Well, not quite everyone. Dr. Amelius Maybury lived close to the Plaza and he took Mr. Spickernell to court claiming under the ancient lights law that the cinema was obstructing his windows. He demanded that part of the western wall be pulled down. After a two day deliberation the judge decided the wall should remain, but that Mr. Spickernell should pay the doctor £70 in costs and compensation.

Disaster struck in the January of 1929: equipment for the new talking films was in the process of being installed when a fire broke out near the projection room and machinery was destroyed to the tune of £3,000. We add that if it had not been for the prompt action of the Portsmouth Fire Brigade the affair would have been a lot worse. The Plaza management also acted quickly. They located the necessary equipment so that the "Singing Fool" could be presented on January 28th. This was the first talking film to be shown in Portsmouth and long queues formed at the Plaza, even outside.

Queues also formed outside on Sunday the 17th of March in 1929. This was for the first Sunday film show presented in Portsmouth. There were quite remarkable scenes outside the Plaza: on the other side of the road an elderly lady surrounded by plenty of supporters was holding a demonstration. Pointing at the Plaza she shouted: "Over there is the Devil's ground' they are all going to a bottomless pit". In the end, the police were forced to move her on. The cinema patrons after waiting for over an hour, filed in to see "Across the Black Country", not appearing to be bothered that they were going to a bottomless pit!

That was not quite the end, because a short time after this affair Frank Spickernell was taken to court yet again and duly summoned for using the cinema for music on a Sunday. Actually, they had used a gramophone instead of the orchestra. He was fined £5, with £20 costs.

And so the Plaza continued as one of Portsmouth's premier cinemas, surviving the war, and the 1950s. But by the end of the 60s this grand picture house was used as a bingo hall, and indeed still carries out this role, standing defiantly on the corner of Bradford Junction. We wonder what that dear old lady would have thought about bingo!

The Southsea Electric - The Fawcett - The Capitol - The Commodore - The State

Cutting through from Bradford Junction, into Fawcett Road, and down to the corner of Bramble Road, before the last war we would have found the picture house we are looking for. It started life as the 'Southsea Electric Theatre' but the name was changed several times in later years.

The doors of the Southsea Electric were opened on September 22nd 1911 and the first film shown to the 700 strong audience was "Always a Way". Well worth the 3d. or 6d. admission charge.

Patrons at the Southsea Electric did even better in the early 20s, for those buying balcony seats for 1/3d. were served cups of tea with biscuits, for free! There was a very popular week's repertoire of films shown in the July of 1924 - each day featured a different Alla Nazimova film. She was the Russian born actress who made her name in Hollywood.

Then followed the changes in name: the Southsea Electric

Opening Day

became 'The Fawcett Picture House'. But it went up for auction in 1929, it fetched over £10,000 and was renamed 'The Capitol'. After several alterations, during which talking equipment was added, this cinema was renamed 'The Commodore'. It then settled down to some happier years in the 30s; a large organ was added, and many happy sing-alongs transpired.

Then in 1938 it became 'The State' and this is the title more people will be familiar with. The State really opened with a bang on the 9th of July: the ceremony being performed by Sir Herbert Cayser, the Conservative M.P. for Portsmouth South. But the highlight was the first programme shown. This was dear old Will Hay in "Oh, Mister Porter", which we film buffs freely admit we could see again and again.

But sorry to say the State only enjoyed another couple of years, for it was closed in 1940 to become a store. It came to life later as the Embassy Ballroom but even dancing was hit by television and the site is now Embassy Court.

The Scala

Down in Elm Grove, in 1920 something stirred. This fashionable Southsea shopping area saw the 'Scala Picture House' erected, near the corner of Yarborough Road. The cinema was built by Messrs. Pannell and the entertainment was managed by the two sons, Gordon and Victor Pannell.

It was a striking looking building, with granite semi-circular arches leading into a tastefully decorated entrance hall. It sported richly upholstered seats in red plush and the flooring was of thick carpet, ensuring comfort for the 700 patrons that it could hold.

It also boasted a fine orchestra, led by Mr. H. Bishop. The first programme starting on Monday the 4th of October 1920 was "A Temporary Vagabond". The Scala was open from 2 o'clock in the afternoon until 10.30pm. It also had a cafe over the vestibule in which patrons and shoppers in Southsea could partake of a cuppa. It may also be added that the Scala had no less than seven sets of lavatory accommodation. Surely the films weren't that bad!

All went well until World War Two. Yes, once again that night of January 10th in 1941. The bombs fell and it was farewell to the Scala in Elm Grove.

The Kings

We will now go on safari into the interior known as Sunny Southsea and what easier than to stroll down Elm Grove and into Albert Road. Now we will enter a thoroughfare that once boasted a good selection of cinemas, but is now left with one such mecca of film entertainment.

We will commence with the 'King's Theatre' which we are

"Scala", Elm Grove

pleased to say still stands proudly on its prominent corner. Younger readers may not realise that although it is a live theatre and has been for many years, the King's did have periods of showing films.

The King's Theatre opened on the 30th of September 1907, built for Portsmouth Theatres Limited. In that first week they provided a feast of acting for the Southsea theatre goer: Mr. H.B. Irving, one of Sir Henry's sons, presented a variety of plays throughout the week. These included "The Bells", "Charles the First" and "The Lyons Mail".

During the following years the theatre continued with stage productions, from straight plays to music hall. There was one particular night in the December of 1912 that will go down in the

King's, Southsea

theatre's history. It was packed to capacity and in fact hundreds were turned away. What was the show? Actually it was a special service in memory of General William Booth, Chief of the Salvation Army. One very prominent member of the audience was Councillor J.E. Smith, later Lord Mayor of Portsmouth. He was a great Salvation Army man, and had four sons and six daughters, all in the Army as well.

Films were beginning to make an impression in the world of entertainment so in the 20s the King's presented film shows in the afternoons, with live music hall bills in the evenings. Then in 1932 films were shown as the main attraction. March 7th of that year saw the start of an all-talkie season, commencing with Constance Bennett in "Common Law", supported by the Pathetone News in sound.

Unlike its sister theatre in Commercial Road, the King's did not have a prolonged spell as a cinema. It survived the bombs of the war, and fortunately it has survived the onslaught of the television medium. We are pleased to report that the management are still presenting the top stage entertainment available today.

Although our interests are as of this moment in the film world, we must stress that it is vital that a theatre with the calibre of the King's should remain open. A working example of Portsmouth's heritage.

The Apollo

We have not got far to go to our next cinema, so this might be a good opportunity for those who wish to quench their thirst to visit the King's Hotel opposite the theatre. For those with more sober tastes, I may suggest a good variety of cafes in the locality.

Ah, there you are! Feeling better now? Then off we go again. On the same side, not many yards from the King's Theatre, we would have found the 'Apollo'. Built of stone and red brick,

"Apollo", Albert Road, Southsea

entrance decorated in white enamel, terrace paving and marble steps. More like a miniature palace, and of course that was the intention - imparting a feeling of grandeur.

The formal opening night was on Monday the 8th of April 1912 and this 500 seater cinema with the title 'Apollo Electric Theatre' emblazoned outside was full to the brim. For the first three days the programme was "A Cure For Jealousy" plus shorts. For the rest of the week the great attraction "Vanity Fair" was shown. Also to full houses.

The audiences continued to pour in and during the following years the Apollo had several extensions added. The success was very much due to the vitality of the management, who were not slow to realise the powers of advertising. The frontage was always well adorned with posters, one such 1923 hoarding

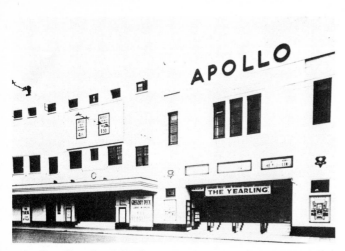

Apollo, Albert Road, Southsea

announcing the showing of the latest sensational production "Custer's Last Stand" and underneath this they proclaimed that film of the Southsea Carnival would also be shown exclusively, hence the capitals: "ARE YOU IN IT?". And we would surmise that many folk went to the Apollo just to see if they were in it!

The coming of the 'talkies' continued to pack them in, and things went smoothly enough through the 30s, the most significant part being in 1939 when Associated British Cinemas took over as proprietors. The Apollo continued into the halcyon cinema days of the post war years, undergoing a change of title to the 'Classic Southsea'. Then in 1975 the crunch came: a notice was placed outside stating that this cinema would close and thanked filmgoers for their past patronage.

Those doors closed on Saturday the 29th of November in 1975 and the last film shown was "The Bruce Lee Story", starring that oriental King of Chop-Socky. So ended the run of another picture house, where never again would audiences laugh at the antics of the little man with the cane and baggy pants, or never again thrill to the adventures of "Strongheart the Wonder Dog". Now just vague memories of the past.

The Gaiety Cinema
Moving up Albert Road towards Eastney, nearing Highland Road Bridge we find 'The Gaiety Cinema'. This was another cinema that started off with a bang on the 5th of February 1924. Not only did they present Holbrook Blinn in "The Bad Man" - Holbrook Blinn? - they also engaged the well known Messy. Sorry, Mezzo Soprano Miss Irene Selwood, to render a few songs accompanied by the Grand Orchestra, directed by Harry Tredgold. All that for just 6d., 9d or 1/- for a balcony seat.

The Gaiety was an imposing building, 170ft. long by 50ft. wide. It could seat 1,100 patrons. Built by Frank Corke, it sported oak pannelled walls to add the feeling of luxury and the ceiling was arched and decorated with ornamental plaster pieces. We may add that one of the exits led out on the slope leading to the Highland Road Bridge that was once part of the Southern Railway spur to Southsea. Alas, now all gone.

An unusual point regarding the old Gaiety was that it had two entrances with two separate pay-boxes. The main one being in Highland Road and the other one being in Henley Road. The Highland Road facia was finished in white atlas cement, with a handsome ornamental canopy complete with hidden lighting.

The Gaiety also changed hands a number of times through its existence, and at one time during the early 30s it came under the A.B.C. chain. By the late 50s it was run by the Portsmouth Town Cinemas, and it was under their proprietorship that this splendid little picture house in Highland Road closed in the January of 1959. The last films shown were "The Spoilers" and "Ma and Pa Kettle at Home". Do you remember that marvellous "Kettles" series of films, with the crusty Marjorie Main and that loveable hayseed Percy Kilbride.

And so the Gaiety closed its doors on the 30th of January and the building that had been another of architect Cogswell's pride and joys was replaced by a supermarket. Around the same period the Curzon Cinema out at Waterlooville was also closed. It also came under Portsmouth Town Cinemas. The Curzon had a relatively short life, being built in the late 1930s.

The Odeon, Southsea
We now look across to the corner of Albert and Festing Roads, where in 1937 the workforce of Messrs. Frank Privett the builders saw the efforts of their labours bear fruit. A massive building with twin terracotta towers heralded the arrival of the 'Odeon', a sister cinema for the one in North End.

The Odeon in Southsea was really the height of luxury; built to accommodate 1,700 customers with ample leg-room. As you entered the pay-desk was in the centre of the foyer on a glass island. This subsequently led into the magnificent auditorium. When they had taken their seats that first audience on the 4th of December saw "The Skys the Limit", with Jack Buchanan. The Lord and Lady Mayoress, Councillor and Mrs. Spickernell, were in attendance, as were the Band of H.M. Royal Marines playing live on stage.

It is interesting that with the building of the Odeon, the fact had been recognised that the horseless carriage was here to stay, for at that time it boasted of having the largest car park in Portsmouth.

Not much more can be added about the Southsea Odeon, except to say that it has undergone a change of name. It still shows the best in cinema entertainment as it has done for the past

Odeon, Southsea

forty years, but it does it under the title of 'The Salon'. Long may it flourish. It is so good to be able to write about a cinema that is still operating.

The Eastney Electric Theatre
Before we turn our feet in a northerly direction, we have one more cinema to visit in the south of the area. It would be a shame to miss 'The Eastney Electric Theatre'. This splendid place of entertainment was opened in 1910 and on October the 10th the first audience saw "Honeymoon for Three", "Out of the Past" and "Marrying Mixture". The price of admission was 2d., 4d. and 6d.

This Eastney Road picture house was built in three months for the proprietors, Messrs. Cook and Bamber. It was described as a high, cool, airy structure, capable of seating 650 patrons.

Bamber and Cook had previously been proprietors of the Shaftesbury in Kingston Road, but very early on let the lease to Messrs. Andrews. But we are afraid the Eastney Electric suffered many changes of ownership. In 1932 it was vastly altered and improved. This included the installation of new sound equipment. Then with a great amount of razamataz, it re-opened as the 'Regal Theatre'.

But this cinema still continued to have changes of ownership, until by the 1950s it was flying under the banner of the Essoldo chain, with the little 'Essoldo Eastney' displayed on its advertising. It was under this name that the doors finally closed in 1963, and so the residents of Eastney lost their cinema after 53 years of good service.

At this stage we will say farewell to Sunny Southsea although we might add that the South Parade Pier showed films at odd occasions, mostly in the 30s. Readers might also remember back to 1964 when a rather strange contraption was erected on the common. This was billed as 'Cinerama' and on a 40ft. high by 120ft. long half-circular screen audiences could witness the wonders of this particular film medium. In a varied programme they were taken on a tour of Europe. They were taken on a roller-coaster, given the feeling of going down a ski-run, followed by a flight across America. Southsea must have seemed a little tame when the audience eventually escaped from this unusual mobile cinema!

Cosham Picture House

We are now heading north. Stop, there is no need to put your snow shoes on! This is to be the north of Portsmouth, namely the fair hamlet of Cosham. A good mode of transport would be the

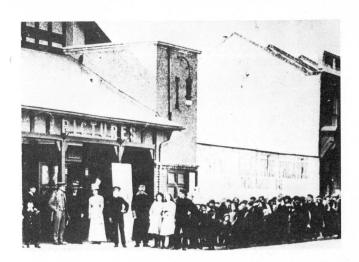

"Eastney Electric"

jolly old train, for as you alight from the train at Cosham Station, and walk to the railway crossing, you will find yourself in the High Street. Now this particular thoroughfare can boast of having three cinemas in the late 30s, all opened at the same time.

Lets start with the oldest cinema, and for this we go back to 1921. That year was notable for Mary Pickford's "Little Lord Fauntleroy", Valentino's "The Four Horsemen of the Apocalypse" and Fairbanks in "The Three Musketeers". It was also the year that the 'Cosham Picture House' opened.

This film establishment had the Woolworth's store on one side of it and the 'George and Dragon' on the other. This was in the

Waverley, Cosham
between George & Dragon and Woolworth's

days when you could buy anything in Woolworth's for 3d. and 6d. and for the same amount you could get quite sloshed in the George and Dragon.

The Grand Opening of the Cosham Picture House took place on the 7th of November in 1921. Lord Mayor, Councillor Timpson did the honours and then they piled in to see "Her Penalty" and "The Amazing Quest of Mr. Bliss". It was a nice touch that on tht first night included in the special guests were three inmates from the Cosham Almshouses. Another good and original touch was that the opening ceremony was filmed with the Lord Mayor and his party and subsequently shown later that week.

Built by Messrs. F. Privett, the Cosham Picture House was in old English - almost Tudor - style of architecture. In fact, it also had a cafe on the first floor, which was aptly named 'The Old Oak Tearooms'.

This picture house was renamed the 'Cosham Cinema' in 1930, and within a few years this was changed to 'The Waverley' in 1934. This was under Mr. F. Olding, and the first programme with its new name was on the 5th of November with "Two Hearts in Spring" starring that old smoothie Carl Brisson.

The Waverley as a cinema did not have to suffer the indignity of bombs being dropped on it for it closed its doors in 1939. So it was exit time for Cosham's first cinema. Never mind, it had two others.

The Carlton

Awfully sorry to march you up and down Cosham High Street but the next cinema is back towards the level crossing gates. Never mind, before the war you could have had a nice pot of tea to wash down delicious cream cakes at Kimbell's Restaurant. This establishment was next door to our next cinema, 'The Carlton'.

Once again, luxurious was the only way to describe this cinema. Imposing white frontage in the modern style, three double doors leading into the carpeted interior. Amidst the plush surroundings a picturesque fountain played. The water sprays are illuminated by a variation of coloured lights. No expense was spared. In fact the cost of the building was £25,000 with £5,000 for extras! That's unusual - we thought only the films had extras!

The opening ceremony was performed on February the 28th 1934 by the one and only Jack Buchanan, riding high at the time with his rendering of "Goodnight Vienna". We suppose as the management had asked him down for the occasion, the only decent thing to do was to show one of his films, which happened to be "That's a Good Girl".

The Carlton carried on for the rest of the 30s until in December of 1940 a bomb fell on it and it was forced to close. That was the bad news; the good news was that it re-opened in the following December.

After the war the Carlton became 'The Essoldo Cosham' and in more recent years that title has changed yet again. It is now called 'The Classic' and still shows top class films from the same site, flying the flag as Cosham's only cinema.

The Ambassador - Odeon

Stop. Just a minute, before you get on the train again, we have one more cinema to visit. We cannot miss 'The Ambassador', even if it is right back down the end of the High Street.

This was one cinema that did not open with "Oh, Mister Porter", in fact it went one better by inviting Will Hay himself to the opening on March the 8th 1937. A large crowd gave Will a tremendous welcome. Then the Lord Mayor Frank Spickernell gave a very humorous speech. In fact it was so funny that in following him Will Hay said that they could have performed a double-act with himself as the straight-man.

The Band of the Royal Marines also played at the opening and organist Thomas Grosch jumped onto the Ambassador's Compton organ, amazing the audience with his "Phantom Piano" novelty item. Oh, we almost forgot. They also showed films. The first being "Dishonour Bright" with Tom Walls, coupled with Richard Dix in "Special Investigator".

Once again, luxury was the name of the game. Anything the Carlton can do, we can do better. A large entrance hall, with two staircases providing access to the balcony and the tea lounge, the latter having the facilities to be quickly converted into a dance floor.

The Ambassador survived the war, but it did not survive a change of name. "Can't Help Singing" with Deanna Durbin on

May 4th 1945 saw that name taken down. But on Sunday May the 6th the name 'Odeon' was fixed to the facia instead. The first film under this new name was "None But The Lonely Heart".

But in recent years even that name has been taken down, the showing of films discontinued and the word 'Bingo' now reigns at that end of the High Street. This is not an entirely happy situation for the avid filmgoer but proprietors can only be led according to the public demands. If bingo is what they want, then that's what they shall have. We tend to hope that the bingo halls are only acting as caretakers for these great buildings, waiting for the day when families will want to go once again to the pictures. Well, we can only hope!

The Alexandra

Right, now you can get on board that train at Cosham Station. That's fine. Rest your weary feet for a little while. I think you deserve it after all that tramping about. Never mind, like Gene Autry, we are heading for the last round-up. So book your train ticket for Fareham Station, for a look at some more good old picture houses.

If things had gone according to plan, we might have been stopping off at Portchester on the way. Before the war Portchester was in the process of becoming a built-up area, with Portsmouth residents moving out of the big city. Parts that had once been fields of green were filling up fast. With this in mind, plans were made in 1937 to build a grand 2,000 seater cinema in Portchester. Unfortunately, these plans faded, so its on we must go to Fareham.

Presuming that we are travelling back in time between 1906 and 1930, for that is the period of time that the electric trams of the Gosport and Fareham Tramways ran, you may get on the tram at the station for the short ride down West Street, to find our first cinema in this market town.

Alexandra, West Street, Fareham

There it is, 'The Alexandra'. In the early part of its history this establishment presented live stage entertainment, but by 1910 moving pictures were also included in the programme. The family name that is associated with the Alexandra is that of the Flemons. Thomas Flemons took it over in its early days, assisted by his good lady wife.

Thomas was a tall distinguished looking gent. Before entering the moving picture business he had built quite a reputation for himself as a still photographer. This was in the Tonbridge area of Kent where he had originated.

Mrs. Flemons worked in the cinema, she was a striking looking woman with long tresses flowing down her back, the colour of which changed at very frequent intervals. In fact, regular patrons were sure the hair was not real. It just had to be a wig! Intent upon finding out, one evening a bunch of soldiers from nearby Fort Fareham went up into the gallery with a fishing line they had improvised. From their perch they tried to hook off Mrs. Flemons' hair whilst she was standing below them. The only snag was, it would not come! It really was her own hair, she must have been a dab hand with hair dye!

The Flemons' son Sidney was also brought into the business, as a projectionist. And his wife Kathleen also worked at the Alexandra, as a pianist. Ray Flemons played the violin at times, along with another lady named Miss Weston. They both had different violins of course, its difficult for two musicians on one violin!

One patron at the Alexandra who could always be sure of having plenty of vacant seats around him was 'Gypsy Joe'. He came in regularly from Titchfield. Sitting in the front row he would shout and laugh like a maniac at everything that appeared on the screen. The staff would dread the showing of cowboy films. Our Romany friend would gallop up and down the aisles!

The Alexandra was completely re-constructed in 1928, which meant that it had to close for a while. But it was re-opened with a great razzamataz; in fact the ceremony was performed by the Rev. Hargrave, the Vicar of Holy Trinity. When you think about it, this was rather unusual - getting a vicar to open a picture house! Anyway, by this period the proprietors were the Fareham and District Entertainments, with Bill Bonwick as managing director. The first film shown in the new super-dooper Alexandra in 1928 was "Annie Laurie" with Lilian Gish. But before the film started the show was opened by the Alexandra Orchestra playing "Land of Hope and Glory". It's great to be British!

In 1929 Mr. Adams the manager of the Alexandra, received a letter from a visitor to Fareham, stating that in his view the cinema was the best he had visited. The seating was good, the prices were low, and the orchestra was better than some he had heard in London. So that was certainly one happy customer.

But all good things come to an end and the end for the Alexandra came in 1933. The last film shown was "Central Airport" with Richard Barthelmess and Sally Eilers. Those great teak doors were closed on December 19th but just down the road another set of cinema doors was opening.

The Savoy

In 1933 Bill Bonwick decided that the Alexandra was just not adequate for a rapidly expanding town such as Fareham, and so plans were drawn up for the erection of Savoy Buildings in West Street. It comprised shops and businesses, and of course a cinema. The latter to be named "The Savoy".

Once again, it was the last word in luxury, providing 1,000 really comfortable seats for its patrons and films projected by the latest and also very expensive Ernimann projectors. The whole cinema project cost £25,000.

The first film show at the Savoy was "Hell Below" with Robert Montgomery and Walter Huston. This set the pace for the film entertainment that was to follow - showing the best films available.

Even so, the Savoy did not enjoy a very long career as a cinema, closing down in the late 50s. The giant Woolworth chain store spread its premises and the Savoy site has been swallowed up in the new Fareham Precinct scheme.

The Embassy

Such was the fever of the cinema days before the last war, another cinema was built in Fareham in 1938 by the S & K Cinema Chain. This was to be called "The Embassy" and it was erected on the site of the old Alexandra, opposite Westbury Manor.

It was opened officially on April 19th 1938 by Captain Manley-Power. (They must have run out of vicars). The privilege for

Savoy, Fareham

43

sitting in this "New luxury cinema" as it was advertised, was paid for by admission charges of 6d, 9d and 1/- for stall seats and 1/3d and 1/6d for circle.

The first film show at the Embassy was "Doctor Syn", starring that fine actor George Arliss, who you may remember gave such a marvellous portrayal in "Disraeli", one of the first talkies.

The Embassy has set something of a record for cinema history in Fareham, for after over 40 years of service it is still going strong in its role as Fareham's only cinema. Long may it continue.

The Picturedrome

It is time to get on board that tram again. So now you can look forward to a very pleasant ride through nearly five miles of countryside; nothing but fields, farms and a few old cottages. Not even a shed with 'Ultra' or 'Fleetlands' marked up on it!

Welcome to Gosport, home of the British Submarines, where Queen Victoria had her very own railway station, and the place of which Cecil B. de Mille once said "Where?".

Well, Gosport had at least six cinemas during the last 70 years and it is at those places of pleasure we shall be having a brief look now.

One of the earliest picture houses in Gosport was "The Picturedrome", this was sited in Avenue Road, close to the Christ Church Institute. It was built of wood and sheets of corrugated iron, previously a Baptist Chapel, it was nicknamed the "Tin Tabernacle".

The roof was mainly corrugated iron and, as the building was 100ft. long by 40ft. wide, you may understand that that was some tin roof. This also accounted for the fact that when it rained, it sounded like Fred Astaire tap-dancing over the patron's heads.

Starting up as a cinema around 1910, the conditions at times were rather crude. In thos days the screen of the Picturedrome was not fireproof so during the intervals a member of staff would stand behind the screen and hose it down with water. This was a

Picture Drome, Avenue Road, Gosport

signal for every small boy in the sudience to pelt the screen with orange peel and apple cores!

Then one fateful Saturday night the Picturedrome caught fire; this was on the 26th of February 1916. Despite the efforts of Fire Chief William Murch and his brave band of chaps, the Picturedrome burnt to the ground. So ended the life of the "Tin Tabernacle". A block of flats known as Avenue Chambers has stood on the site for many years.

The Olympia

Next to Avenue Road the following turning off Stoke Road is Queens Road. On the corner of Queens Road stood one of Gosport's most revered picture houses. Older Gosport residents will at once shout "The Olympia" and of course they will be correct.

Olympia, Stoke Road, Gosport

Staff - Olympia, Stoke Road, Gosport

This building started off life as a roller skating rink in 1910 but by 1914 moving films had taken over. As far as roller skating went anyway, the films still had to share the entertainment with live stage acts. One of which was "Omo - the Tattooed Man" - I bet with a name like that he must have had a clean act!

The early Olympia also had a tin roof and there were also other hazards in the rainy season. The water would drain down the slope of the cinema and form great puddles at the orchestra pit end. This was so bad at times that the musicians would play with their feet on chairs.

Young mums attending the afternoon matinees with babies in arms were a bit of a menace, when baby got fidgety they would change its nappy in the dark. Then they would drape the nappies over the cinema radiators to dry! It is quite understandable that mum would get so carried away with Rudolph Valentino galloping across the desert on his camel, she would forget to take the nappy home when the programme had finished.

The name associated with the Olympia was that of the Horne family. Ted Horne was the manager and his brother Steve was the projectionist. Their father was the actual proprietor. Steve Horne was assisted by two brothers, Alf and Ernie Poulton, who put in over 20 years at this cinema. And just to keep it in the family, there were three Poulton sisters who were on the staff as usherettes.

The Olympia had a most formidable doorman in the shape of Jack Green, a proper sargeant-major of a man who proudly displayed his war medals across his uniform. When the audience got noisy he would stride up and down the aisles shouting "Quiet please"

When the talkies came in the Olympia was very much altered and modernised. A quieter roof was fitted and the entrance was changed from the corner and resited square in Stoke Road. But by 1935 the end was near, the doors closed and the building became a furniture repository. It became a dilapidated hulk to be finished off by Hitler's bombs in World War Two. The site has remained dormant ever since but in recent months builders have moved in and dwellings are at present in course of erection.

The Gosport Theatre

Gosport's main thoroughfare, the High Street, can only boast one cinema. Although in 1919 plans were made to build another cinema in this street. It was to be called "The Victory House", incorporated in a complex of flats, tearooms and roof gardens, all providing excellent views over the harbour and Spithead. But the plans were shelved and so Gosport lost a 1,000 seater luxury cinema.

But it did have the "Gosport Theatre" in the High Street. This had previously been a chapel of the Wesleyan Church, but in 1910 it was converted into a picture house. A splendid place it was too; decorated to provide a warm homely atmosphere for its patrons.

The proprietors were the Gosport Bioscope Company and once again the usual format of early cinemas was put into practice: live stage entertainment with the films. In 1911 the inmates of the House of Industry (Workhouse) were specially invited by the management to a special showing of King George V's Coronation at Westminster Abbey. Needless to say, the inmates were delighted, and could not stop talking about it for weeks.

Gosport Theatre

Mr. H. Romain was manager of the Gosport Theatre around 1923, and it was during that time that live stage drama was introduced regularly. This was performed by the Grant Anderson Stock Company, presenting melodrama in the 'cheer the hero, boo the villian' style.

This cinema came under new management in 1928, guess who took it over? Yes, our old friend Bill Bonwick, who appeared to have a finger in every cinema pie in those days! Bill appeared to own cinemas like suits but he also found time to stand in the Gosport Borough Council elections in 1930. And won!

In 1929 the Gosport Theatre was the centre of a court case. American and European films were being booked at cinemas before they were registered in this country for showing. The European Film Company of Wardour Street were accused by the Board of Trade of this practice. Bill Bonwick was called to give evidence that bookings for a film title "Danger River" were

Escapeologist -
Gosport Theatre, High Street - 1910c

First staff of Gosport Theatre, High Street - 1910c

47

taken for the 27th of August 1929, when in actual fact the film was not registered until November the 9th. The film company was given a strong warning to cease this practice, and were fined a small amount of money.

The Gosport Theatre carried on for many years dolling out large doses of film entertainment, but it was to close its doors forever in 1938. That foyer which welcomed patrons so warmly is now the site of Rumbelows electrical shop, but the main hall is still fairly intact, serving as auction rooms for Messrs. Coates.

The Ritz

If we were to stroll up the High Street, past the old Thorngate Hall, we would come to the start of Walpole Road. On one side of this road was the old library and secondary school, and on the opposite side is the Conservative Club, opened in 1914. Next to this building, where the old ramparts once ran through, is the building we are looking for: "The Ritz".

On one Spring day in March 1935, a large crowd assembled in Walpole Road. A cheer went up as a party of well-dressed gents arrived on the scene, and even more cheers when Mr. Lofts the Chairman of Portsmouth Town Cinemas introduced Leslie Henson the well known revue comedian. Leslie had the crowd in fits with his humorous speech then he declared the Ritz well and truly open.

The first film shown was "What Every Woman Knows" and that was just the start of the wonderful string of films to followed. In the first year the Ritz presented "The Lives of a Bengal Lancer", "The Scarlet Pimpernel", "Sanders of the River", "David Copperfield" and "Bright Eyes", just to name a few. One very interesting fact is that the Gosport Ritz could boast of staging the British premiere of "Captains Courageous", that classic movie starring Spencer Tracy.

Ritz, Gosport

In 1935 the Ritz was a marvel of modern architecture, with futuristic decor to match. Not only did the 1,000 patrons that this cinema would hold have luxurious seats, they could also partake of morning coffee, dainty teas and light suppers in the Ritz Cafe. This cafe also pronounced the wonders of its speciality, a 3-course luncheon for 1/6d. This was very popular. We dare to venture that it would be even more popular now, at that price anyway!

In the first year of the Ritz, over half a million people went to the pictures there and if all the tickets issued were laid end to end they would go fifty times around H.M.S. Nelson, the great battleship of that time.

If you thought leaving baby's nappies was bad enough, the Ritz takes the prize for lost property. In one year the following were left behind: 1,000 gloves, a pig's trotter, two rabbits (dead), a set of false teeth, and would you believe, one live baby!

Within a few years disaster was to strike at the Ritz; yes, that fateful night of the war again. Bombs and incendiary missiles reduced the building to a burnt out shell. That was the bad news, the good news being that it was rebuilt and opened again in the 1950s. In fact, it still reigns as Gosport's only cinema, and there has been talk of it being converted into a two-screen cinema in recent times. This would be a very exciting venture for the town's film fans we are sure.

The Forum

What marvellous cinema days in Gosport they were in thos pre-war years, when the picture house was an establishment of stature in society. And what is more it was available to all classes of society.

A good tale to illustrate this is related by Basil Tucker, who as a young chap acted as assistant manager at one time or another in most of the area's cinemas. He recalls those days of the 1930s when the phone would ring and a voice at the other end would say "This is Admiral So-and-so of Alverstoke. I have a dinner party of ten guests and would like to reserve seats for this evening's performance". The Admiral and his party would duly arrive complete with evening dress and bow ties, to be ushered to their 1/10d. seats!

Basil can also add to our lists of lost property left in cinemas: two housebricks, wallets with pornographic photos and several pairs of knickers! You may not be surprised to learn that these articles were seldom claimed! He also tells us that the playing of "Tipperary" at the Ritz was the signal for the staff to open all doors if there was a fire.

But we digress. Replacing the Olympia in Stoke Road in the 1930s was another picture house, a really super-dooper structure that went under the banner of "The Forum". But 1939 was hardly the best time to open a cinema anywhere in this country.

The Forum was built on the corner of Shaftesbury Road and Stoke Road, on a site that had previously housed Groom's Nurseries, Stoke House and Stoke Lodge. Built on modern lines, it was a most impressive building inside and out. But apart from the outbreak of war, the chips seemed stacked against this cinema from the start. The first manager Mr. Holland had hardly been instated in his new office when he had to go to court to give evidence against two 13-year-old lads who were both fined for slashing seats with a knife at the Forum.

After the Ritz was bombed and subsequently closed, the Forum enjoyed good patronage for a number of years, but when the Ritz was re-opened the rot began to set in and the Forum was closed in the late 1950s. It was converted into a car showroom and petrol station, which in turn was demolished. The site now houses the large Waitrose Supermarket. And so ended the history of the Forum, being able to claim the dubious title of being the shortest running purpose built cinema in the Gosport area.

The Criterion

We have one more cinema to visit in Gosport, and for this we will have to venture over to the Forton area of town. When we state that we are standing by the crossroads in Forton Road, many readers will have realised we are paying a visit to the old 'Criterion'.

Built on the site of the old Admiralty Waterworks, the Criterion was opened on May the 8th in 1912. This was in the presence of many distinguished guests, including representatives of the Magisterial Bench and other bodies. The films shown in the first programme were more of a documentary type, including "With Our King and Queen Through India" and "Scenes in Delhi".

Anyway, it was much appreciated by the first day audience, who were also treated to tea and refreshments. Stage shows were also presented with the bioscope items, and of course it had the usual orchestra. One of the most popular pianists at the 'Old Cri' was Miss Ada Lyne, but she also did some moonlighting to play at other cinemas. Ada married one of the doormen, and as Mrs. Smith she formed the famous Sunshine Kiddies in later years.

Ada's sister also worked at the Criterion in the pay-box out front. She married Mr. Penfold the projectionist, so you can imagine it was a very happy cinema. By the 20s it was also acquired by Bill Bonwick, who we warned you at the start would crop up at regular intervals. During this period he also owned the Arcade Cinema in Portsmouth.

The Criterion continued with its filmfare through the 30s, and came through the war fairly well. Although there is one wartime memory worth relating from our old friend Basil Tucker. He was standing in the entrance of the Criterion when a bomb dropped between Forton Church and Crosslands, the Undertakers. Basil rushed into the cinema where about 100 patrons were seated. There was no panic, but he was just in time to see Fred Astaire and Ginger Rogers dancing on the side curtains instead of the screen! The projector had been jolted off its moorings but was still turning!

The Criterion was still packing them in after the war, and on into the 1960s. But in the end, like many others, it was converted into a bingo hall and is indeed still thriving under the title 'Crown Bingo'. Recently, thanks to the courtesy of the management, we were able to take a close look at the Criterion building. Top marks to the proprietors, the old trappings have been retained to a great extent. It is tastefully decorated and looks as if it could be converted back into a cinema at a moment's notice. But of course, although it has Crown Bingo on the facia, it is still referred to by most locals as 'The Old Cri'.

CRITERION THEATRE

FORTON ROAD, GOSPORT

Proprietor and Manager: W. BONWICK

'Phone No.: Gosport 8128

A Modern Theatre. Orchestral Music.

Comfortable Seats. First-class Projection.

The Latest Productions Screened.

Criterion, Gosport

Fred Weaver - Chocolate Boy
Criterion, Gosport

The Tower Cinema

Like us, you must be getting pretty weary by now. We have just one more cinema from the past to visit, and what better than a breath of sea air to revive us. This particular cinema must have surely been on the most glorious site in the country, affording fantastic sea views over the Solent and the Isle of Wight. Its title was simply 'The Tower' and its position was in that splendid area of Gosport known as Lee-on-Solent.

The Tower cinema and its complex was built in 1935 for Solent Properties by local builder, Arthur Prestige, and the proprietors were determined to make it the envy of every seaside resort in the South Coast. They certainly did their best, for there could not be many picture houses in the country with a 120ft. high tower perched on top of it.

This 900-seater cinema was opened by Admiral Sir Arthur Waistall, assisted by the Mayor of Gosport on December 26th 1935. Yes, Boxing Day again. The first film shown was "Marry the Girl" starring Sonnie Hale, supported by "In Town Tonight" with Stanley Holloway. The admission charges were 6d., 9d. and 1/- for stalls, or 1/6d. and 1/10d. up in the circle.

But within a year the Tower buildings were in trouble. Agents Young and White put it on their boards, and various parts were leased off, including the cinema. This was taken over by a large local cinema chain, and under their guidance it flourished as a picture house for many years. The rest of the Tower complex was acquired by the Gosport Council in 1939 for £55,000 but this proved to be not such a bargain as they had hoped.

Into the war, the Tower building was used for various purposes by the military, including American Forces at one time. We would also surmise that the tower was much appreciated by the German Airforce, making a marvellous landmark!

But the cinema business was falling off by 1958 and that was the year that the Tower Cinema closed. Several types of entertainment were tried in its place, and the once splendid cinema hall was subjected to various spectacles, including all-in wrestling, bingo and ten-pin bowling. They were all to no avail, as history has shown, the complex was demolished in the late 1960s and has been replaced by a glorified carpark. The remarkable fact is that Lee-on-Solent has expanded greatly since then, the residents are crying out for a Community Centre for their needs, yet ten years ago they had one of the finest buildings they could possibly ask for. Oh well, thats life!

We come to the end of the show

Here it is, the moment you have all waited for: "The End". Books such as this are rather like films, when the words "The End" appear you can either feel glad or sorry. We sincerely hope your feelings are the latter.

As you can imagine, a subject such as the cinemas of Portsmouth presented a most formidable task, indeed we do not pretend that we have covered it to its full extent, but at the same time humbly submit that we have probably presented more than has ever been written before on this particular form of entertainment in our area.

Apart from the enjoyment which proprietors appeared to gain from changing the cinemas' names at regular periods, many cinemas closed nearly as soon as they opened. These we have not included. Our one dread whilst preparing this was that yet another cinema would close, in fact as this typewriter is being pounded, the Palace in Guildhall Walk has iron shutters fixed across its facia.

So that is it, the final curtain is falling! Readers can now relax and perhaps think about their own memories relating to cinemas of their past. As for we dedicated film buffs, we shall now put our feet up and dream about winning the football pools. What would we do with the money? That's easy! We would take over an old picture house, call it "The Bijou" and show film seasons that included a fair dose of Shirley Temple, Rudolph Valentino, Humphrey Bogart, Greta Garbo, Errol Flynn, Alice Faye, Fred Astaire, Ginger Rogers, etc. etc...... As Bugs Bunny would say "Brrr. Brrr. That's All Folks!"

Interior - Princes Theatre, Lake Road, Portsmouth

"Arnold's Electric Bioscope"
Portsdown Hill Fair - 1910c

53

Carlton, Cosham
with Kimbell's Cafe

54

Essoldo, Eastney

1

2

3

4

1. *Great expectations outside the Gosport 'Criterion', 1921.*

2. *Staff of Gosport 'Ritz', advertising "Things to Come", 1936.*

3. *Theatre Royal, Portsmouth. Currently being restored.*

4. *'Ritz' restaurant, 1935. 3-course lunch 1/6d.*

5. *The old 'Alexandra', Fareham. 1910c.*

6. *The 'Forum', Stoke Road, Gosport.*

7. *'Victoria Hall', Portsmouth. Will we ever see audiences like this again?*

TWINKLING TOES AND TALENTED TONSILS

FRED ASTAIRE

Mister Twinkle-toes himself, born in Nebraska U.S.A. in 1899, family name Frederick Austerlitz. After considerable success as a dancing team with his sister Adele, he broke into films in 1933, and the same year formed a screen partnership with Ginger Rogers that will stand for all time as a highlight in the history of the cinema.

Apart from his brilliant dancing, he had a singing voice that can only be classed as unique, half-spoken, half-sung, but getting away with songs that others find difficult to copy.

Best films: 'Flying Down to Rio' 1933, 'Top Hat' 1935, 'Blue Skies' 1946, 'Easter Parade' 1948.

GINGER ROGERS

Born in 1911, real name Virginia McMath. Started in films in 1930, and soon made her mark as a dancer, actress, and comedienne. Will always be associated for the musicals that she made with Astaire, but it is often forgotten that she also turned in some fine dramatic roles. Ginger has also enjoyed a good deal of success on the stage, notably in 'Mame', and 'Hello Dolly'.

Best films: '42nd Street' 1933, 'Flying Down to Rio' 1933, 'Roxie Hart' 1942, 'The Major and the Minor' 1942, 'Storm Warning' 1949.

BING CROSBY

Born in 1903, started singing in dance bands such as the Paul Whiteman outfit, and soon won fame for his relaxed style that started the craze for crooning.

Teamed up with comedian Bob Hope and the glamorous Dorothy Lamour, to make many films in the 'Road' series. It is doubtful if ever his like will be seen or heard again, his name along with Jolson will forever rank as one of the greatest entertainers of all time.

Best films: 'Pennies from Heaven' 1936, 'East Side of Heaven' 1939, 'Going My Way' 1944, 'White Christmas' 1954.

SHOOTING STARS

TOM MIX

Born in 1880, Mix was a U.S. Marshal who turned actor in 1914, and starred in 400 low-budget westerns. His original steed was 'Old Blue' but he later acquired his faithful and talented horse 'Tony', so beginning a partnershiip that endured itself to millions.

Mix had a better relationship with horses than with wives, for he was 'roped' to five of the latter. He was killed in a car crash in 1940 at the age of 59.

Best films: 'The Last Trail' 1927, 'Destry Rides Again' 1927, 'The Terror Trail' 1933.

GENE AUTRY

King of the singing cowboys, born in 1907. Often shot by baddies, the ones in the black hats, or burnt at the stake by Indians, but still came back yodelling for more, and of course, still wearing his sparkling white stetson. Made more than 90 cowboy pictures, mostly 'B' category, and generally had with him his hornery old side-kick, Smiley Burnette, plus 'Champion, the Wonder Horse'.

Best films: 'In Old Santa Fe' 1934, 'Mystery Mountain' 1934.

ROY ROGERS

Born in 1912, real name Leonard Slye. Came to prominence in the 1940s, taking over as the 'singing cowboy' when Autry joined the Air Force during the war.

Rogers made over 90 westerns, most of them with his real-life wife Dale Evans, old side-kick Gabby Hayes, and of course the almost human horse, Trigger.

Rogers still appears on television occasionally, notably a guest spot on the 'Muppet Show'.

Best films: 'Along the Navajo Trail' 1946, 'Roll on Texas Moon' 1947, 'Son of Paleface' 1952.

THE TOUGH GUYS

HUMPHREY BOGART

Well loved screen tough guy, born on Christmas Day 1899. Came from an upper-class background, his father was a doctor of note.

Bogart's first film was 'A Devil With Women' in 1930, he lived up to this title, having married four times, his last wife being actress Lauren Bacall.

Made 75 films, and is well remembered for his roles as a gangster, combining well with Cagney. Died of cancer in 1957.

Best films: 'Angels With Dirty Faces' 1938, 'High Sierra' 1941, 'Maltese Falcon' 1941, 'African Queen' 1952.

JAMES CAGNEY

The greatest little tough guy on the screen, born in 1899. Came out of the New York slums, and with his cocky walk and personality, quickly went from vaudeville into films.

Played many roles in his long career, but really shone in gangster parts, although displaying a good line in song and dance routines when called for. Probably the most impersonated star of all time.

Best films: 'Steel Highway' 1930, 'Each Dawn I Die' 1939, 'The Roaring Twenties' 1939, 'Yankee Doodle Dandy' 1942.

GEORGE RAFT

Born in 1895, smooth leading man of the 30s and 40s, came from a tough East Side background. Came to prominence as a night club dancer, and was extremely successful thanks to his style and Valentino looks.

Entered films in 1929, and made his mark in the 1932 gangster movie 'Scarface' with Paul Muni. His main part in the film was to toss a coin in the air, with very little to say, but it was enough to set him on the road to stardom.

Best films: 'Scarface' 1932, 'The Bowery' 1933, 'The Glass Key' 1935, 'Each Dawn I Die' 1939.

THE GODDESS'S

GRETA GARBO

GRETA GARBO
*Became the goddess of the screen, born
in Sweden, 1905. Although she has not
made a film since 1941, she has remained
a cult figure, created mostly through
the air of mystery that has always surrounded her.*

*Her early retirement from films amazed
the world, for at that time she was a top
box-office attraction. But apart from her
aloof beauty, on viewing her acting
prowess in her old films, one might
contemplate that perhaps she made the
right decision.*
*Best films: 'Anna Christi' 1930,
'Grand Hotel' 1932, 'Camille' 1936.*

JEAN HARLOW
*Born in Kansas 1911, Harlean
Carpentier real name. She was probably
Hollywood's most sensational star of the
20s and 30s.*

*Jean had a short life but a merry one,
indulging in three husbands, and exces-
sive quantities of alcohol and male
companionship. Life finally caught up
with her and she died in 1937 at the ripe
old age of 26! But as a cult figure,
this 'blond bombshell' lives on.*
*Best films: 'Hell's Angels' 1930, 'Din-
ner at Eight' 1933, 'China Seas' 1935.*

MARLENE DIETRICH
*German actress who became a legend in
her own lifetime, born Maria Magdalena
von Losch in 1901. Came to prominence
in 'The Blue Angel' as the sexy lady who
led Emil Jannings a dance, and in the
following years she made several films
in the States, some good, but many of
them 'stinkers'. But like Garbo, she has
continued to attract good publicity, and
despite her gravel-singing voice, has
made millions of dollars in cabaret.*
*Best films: 'The Blue Angel' 1930,
'Morocco' 1930, 'The Garden of Allah'
1936, 'Destry Rides Again' 1939.*

THE SWASHBUCKLERS

RUDOLPH VALENTINO

The greatest romantic idol of all time, born in 1895 in Italy. Went to America to seek his fortune, and after a varied career as a restaurant washer-upper and dance-hall gigalo, finally got into films and made women's hearts flutter all over the world.

Not great shakes as an actor, but his agility and good looks got him through. Also enjoyed a goodly amount of publicity, and when he died in 1926, the funeral scenes attracted scenes that would have been more in keeping with royalty.

Best films: 'The Four Horsemen of the Apocalypse' 1921, 'The Sheik' 1921, 'Blood and Sand' 1922.

ERROL FLYNN

Handsome swashbuckler, who's private life was often more thrilling than his films. Born in Tasmania in 1909, he went to Hollywood via a short spell in English Rep., and became known for his dashing escapades whilst playing pirates, forest outlaws, and American war heroes.

Off the screen he indulged in bad marriages, love affairs, law suits, drugs, drink, and general hell-raising. He finally sowed his last wild oat in 1959, after putting into 50 years what would take most people 150!

Best films: 'Captain Blood' 1935, 'The Adventures of Robin Hood' 1938, 'They Died With Their Boots On' 1941, 'The Sun Also Rises' 1957.

DOUGLAS FAIRBANKS

A famous swashbuckler, who was the son of an even more famous swashbuckler. Had a debonair manner that could capture ladies' hearts, and an athletic ability that made most men envious. Born in 1907 in America, but displayed an immaculate English accent.

Married to actress Joan Crawford at one time, and spent a good deal of time in Britain. In the 1950s he made innumerable half-hour shows for television.

Best films: 'The Dawn Patrol' 1930, 'The Prisoner of Zenda' 1937, 'Gunga Din' 1939, 'Sinbad the Sailor' 1947.

THE CHILD STARS

SHIRLEY TEMPLE

"On the good ship, Lollipop", sang this dimpled-cheeked child star, and who could resist her?

Born in 1928, Shirley's first film was "The Water Babies" in 1932, and despite all the publicity during her early career, success never went to her head.

Married actor John Agar in 1947, divorced in 1950, and married husband No. 2 Charles Black. Turned her back on movies, and later became the American Ambassador to Ghana.

Best known of her 55 films: 'Bright Eyes' 1934, 'The Little Colonel' 1935, 'Heidi' 1937, 'Rebecca of Sunnybrook Farm' 1938.

MICKEY ROONEY

Born in 1920, he co-starred in five early musicals with Judy Garland, plus many films in the famous Andy Hardy series.

Rooney developed a habit of collecting wives like most people collect gas bills, one of his more notable marriages being to actress Ava Gardner.

Now no longer in the bloom of youth, he has earnt a reputation as a fine character actor in films and television.

Best early films: 'Huckleberry Finn' 1939, 'Captains Courageous' 1937, 'National Velvet' 1945.

JUDY GARLAND

Volatile child star of Hollywood musicals, born into the business in 1922, her parents being vaudeville performers. First went onto the stage at 5 years old, and from thereon never stopped acting, on or off stage and screen.

Held audiences better than she did husbands, marrying five times. Died from a drugs overdose in 1969, thus ending a sad and tragic life.

Best films: 'The Wizard of Oz' 1939, 'Broadway Melody' 1938, 'Meet Me In St. Louis' 1944, 'Easter Parade' 1948, 'A Star Is Born' 1954.

Is this you – or your Estate Agent?

Saving the £500 – £1000 your estate agent would charge to sell an average house or flat could buy you a superb holiday for two. Instead of paying for your estate agent's holiday, you could sell your property through Homeline – at a cost of around £60.

With Homeline, you can sell privately and discreetly, highlighting the features that mean most to you. There are no hidden extras, and no commission on sale.

For buyers the service is free – you give us your requirements, and we'll send you details of properties that match, putting you in touch with the seller direct.

The Homeline service helps you with surveys, mortgages and conveyancing – in fact everything you need when you move. We have offices throughout the Midlands, the West, the South, and the London area. For more information Phone Portsmouth 833131

PORTSMOUTH 833131

3 Charter House, Lord Montgomery Way, Portsmouth PO1 2SB.

Homeline

The real alternative to estate agents. And their fees.